LIFE BEHIND BARS

Looking Back At My Working Life

Gordon Culpin

Published by Paragon Publishing, Rothersthorpe
First published 2022

© Gordon Culpin, 2022

The rights of Gordon Culpin to be identified as the author of this work have been asserted by him in accordance with the Copyright, Designs and Patents Act of 1988.

All rights reserved; no part of this publication may be reproduced, stored in a retrieval system, or transmitted in any form or by any means, electronic, mechanical, photocopying, recording or otherwise without the prior written consent of the publisher or a licence permitting copying in the UK issued by the Copyright Licensing Agency Ltd. www.cla.co.uk

This book is sold subject to the condition that it shall not, by way of trade or otherwise, be lent, re-sold, hired out or otherwise circulated in any form of binding or cover other than that in which it is published and without a similar condition including this condition being imposed on the subsequent publisher.

ISBN 978-1-78222-962-9

Book design, layout and production management by Into Print
www.intoprint.net
+44 (0)1604 832149

⛓ Foreword ⛓

Some years ago, when talking to family and friends, I was told I should write a book about my working life. At the time I did not see the point, as nobody would be interested. I thought it was a working life just like most other people had. Apparently this was not the case, and I kept being told that my experiences were so varied and interesting.

So, with a lot of persuasion, I made a start, speaking into a recording machine, having it played back and typed on to a computer. Expensive and boring, so I stopped. Later, my son Sam introduced me to a speech recognition program, where I just spoke into a microphone attached to a computer, which produced it in a written word on A4 sheet. As a result, the book was finally completed. I could have had it proofread and edited but I was adamant I wanted it to be me, my words and my life. So, that is what you have got. I am sorry if it does not meet your standards.

I would like to say thank you to my family and friends for putting up with my constant references to my working life, especially Wendy, who I know got bored to tears with hearing about my life, time and time again. Also, the long hours I was at work when, maybe, I should have spent more time at home with her and the kids.

The reason I have called the book *"My Life Behind Bars"* is because I feel we all live behind bars, some you can see, some are in a mist, like an open prison.

Contents

Looking Back	7
Military Service	11
Oil Exploration	27
Between Jobs	39
Dover Borstal	51
HMP Elmley	91
HMP Aldington	97
HMP Northward	107
Taken Hostage	129
Riot	141
Back Home	155

🔗 Looking Back 🔗

I was born in Hayes, Kent in 1941. In 1944 we were bombed out; we were lucky to get out of the house alive. If it had not been for my father building a bomb shelter under the kitchen table, we would not have been alive today. The whole building collapsed, and we had to be dug out. As a result, mother and three kids were evacuated to Lancashire. This was not a pleasant experience and we later moved back to my grandmother's house in Bromley, a few miles from Hayes, until after the war when our old house was rebuilt

In 1947 we moved to Folkestone where my parents opened a 9-bedroom guesthouse. The whole family slept in one room in the summer when we had guests. As soon as us kids were old enough, we had to help around the house and garden. I remember doing my first washing up when I was six. The garden was very large with a large greenhouse, fruit trees veg patches and runs and hutches for chickens, ducks and rabbits. This was all needed because rationing was still on, and food was hard to get. I travelled miles just to queue for hours to get fish, tinned meat and other essential food for us and the guests. Sweets were like gold, only quarter of an ounce per week per person!

The first time I earnt money was at the age of nine when I became a choir boy at St John's Church, Folkestone. We would earn extra money for singing at weddings and other services. During the next three years I was privileged to sing in St Paul's Cathedral, Westminster Abbey and Canterbury Cathedral; and earnt a regular sum to supplement my pocket money (which I also had to work for). Then, sometime after my 12th birthday, the church found out that I was not christened and told my father that unless I was christened, I would have to leave the choir. My father was not keen for me to be christened and so, if the loyalty and service I had given them over three years was not enough, then I would leave.

My first proper employment began in 1954 when I was just thirteen years old. I got a job as a delivery boy for the local grocer's shop. The pay was six-pence an hour, 2½ pence in new money. Legally, I was only allowed to work 8 hours a week, but during the school holidays I often worked more than 30 hours; giving me a massive £1.00 for a week's work. A lot of money for a schoolboy in those days. I travelled miles on a fixed geared bicycle delivering groceries all around Folkestone. If there were lots of deliveries to the same area, I would pull a four-wheeled barrow piled high full of boxes of groceries; just like Granville in the TV series, *Open All Hours.*

When not on delivery duties, I helped around the shop, especially on the outside greengrocer section. In those days most food had to be weighed and measured and the cost had to be added up in your head. There was no adding up tills, just a single money drawer. Very little food was pre-packed, and I even learnt to bone a side of bacon and cut down a whole cheese. When I look back at this time, I realise that it was here that I learnt to communicate and joke with the people I met. There was never a dull moment, both in the shop or when I was out on deliveries; I quickly learnt to be able to talk to people of all ages.

As a schoolboy I was very independent, quiet, but I could look after myself especially against the school bullies. On meeting one of my old teachers a few years ago, he said, "I remember you, because you always replied, "Yes, please sir", when I asked, "does anyone want the cane?"". I had worked out that there was little they could do to punish you if you volunteered for the usual punishment.

In 1957, I was due to leave school and the manager of the shop offered me a job. I would leave school with no formal qualifications, and he was keen to train me to become the manager one day. What was I going to do? Yes, I could have taken the job in the shop and may have made a manager one day. However, my father had taught me many skills like plumbing and woodwork, and I hoped my skills and hardworking attitude would be an asset for me in the future. I really wanted to learn a trade but there were no apprenticeships available around Folkestone in a trade that I was interested in. I saw an advertisement for the Army and noticed that they were recruiting fifteen-year-old boys to join an Army Apprentice School. It offered a three-year apprenticeship in a trade of your choice, along with military training. At the end of three years, you would become a qualified tradesman and a soldier, something which really interested me. My parents were not very happy about this. My brother had joined the Navy three years earlier and their second son looked like he was also going to leave home as well. However, they said it was up to me and that I should make my own pathway in life. I had never been away from home before as we did not have holidays with my parents were running a guest house most of the time. Sometimes I went and stayed with relatives during the summer holidays but, other than that, I had been house-bound. So, this was going to be a big adventure for me.

⛓ Military Service ⛓

In August 1957, after passing the Army's entrance exam, I left home carrying a small suitcase with plimsolls strapped to the outside and made my way to Chepstow in South Wales. That was to be my base for the next three years. What an eye-opener this was!

We were met by this huge Sergeant at the railway station in Chepstow who marched us to the local bus stop and then took us to the camp about three miles away. Within a very short time we were issued with all our kit, given an army number and told to stamp or sew on tags to identify all our equipment. From then on, if we lost something we would have to pay for it. Next, I was allocated to a barrack room with thirty other young boys. I had been propelled from my own bedroom to a huge barrack room, with lines of beds and a coal stove in the middle as the only heating. We were only allowed one bucket of coal per week which was nowhere near enough during the colder winters. Fortunately, we found a way of getting more coal. It required one of us to climb around the riverbank and collect coal from the coal yard which ran alongside the river, which we then hid under the floorboards. We were allowed to use the stoves, but each week they had to be polished for inspection. The grate had a lino insert which had to be spit and polished.

I would describe the food they gave us as only being fit for pigs. It looked, and was served up, Charles Dickens style; mostly scraps of food. It was a real struggle for quite some time and completely out of my normal experience and I lost nearly a stone in weight in less than a month. I knuckled down and after the first six month, I started to enjoy it, despite the intimidation by NCOs and senior trainees who took great pride in trying to bully us. It just went over my head. If I was going to succeed, I would have to take it in my stride, so I concentrated on learning and soon got myself involved in all sorts of activities. Opportunities opened for me in various sports, such as hockey, canoeing and boxing. I was not really interested in boxing, but I found out that if you boxed you got up early, did your training, and went for a late breakfast which was always far better than the others got.

Each term we would spend a few days and nights on the Brecon Beacons. We had to make our tents out of two ponchos. There were no sleeping bags issued, so we had to take the blankets off our beds; not very good when it rained, but we learn to make do. At the end of each term, we had home leave, for which they gave 5 shilling a day food allowance. On return from leave all 800 of us would have to line up in the gymnasium in front of the nurse and drop our trousers and pants to show if we had any diseases around our private parts.

Military Service

I had joined up to train as a plumber, but after seeing the other trades available I had changed my choice to electrician. I then found out my colour blindness would prevent me from do this, so, deciding that modern plumbing was not for me, it had to be mechanics. Being an army mechanic, you had to be trained in various other trades such as welding, fitting and electrics. When you are out in the wilds repairing vehicles, you do not have all these other trades to back you up. I could be called upon to work on anything from a motorbike to tank. In the last year of my training, I was told that, if I came in the first six in the final exams, I would be able to apply for the Army Air Corps. I came fifth out of 80 boys. What they did not tell me was that, because of my colour blindness, I would not be able to join. A vehicle mechanic was what I would be, a trade I enjoyed for the next 20 years.

By 1959 I had reached a high standard of fitness and, as a result, I was selected to go on an Army outward-bound course in North Wales. It was a course only a few were selected to go on each year and so I was very proud of it. It meant spending a month up on the mountains of Snowdonia and the hillsides and coast around Towyn and I thoroughly enjoyed the hard work. While on the course, I was taught rock climbing by a team of instructors, which included Chris Bonington, the well-known mountaineer, who was stationed there at the time. During the final week we were split up into groups of four to map read around the Welsh mountains. We covered nearly 40 miles in two days, sleeping under

Military Service

the stars for two nights; the first night in a layby and the next night in a barn full of cows. It was very strenuous but, because of my map reading skills, we were able to complete the course in under the allotted time.

This training made a man of me. I had joined the Army as a timid little boy and was now a fully grown 18-year-old man and I was very grateful for it. I represented the Apprentice School in athletics and hockey many times. On completion of my boy service in August 1960, I was posted to Germany as a qualified mechanic in the Royal Electrical and Mechanical Engineers, or REME as it was called. Germany was where I was going to spend most of my Army service. I travelled to Germany, first by troopship from Harwich to the Hook of Holland, and then by train down through Germany. They used a novel way of selecting where you got off, such as, "Who plays football?", and those who put their hands up disembarked. They never mentioned hockey, so I stayed on the train until there was only a few of us left and we disembarked at Dortmund. The barracks was on a disused airfield.

Within days I was selected as a member of the regimental hockey team and went on two tours of Berlin. The first visit, in 1960, was before the Berlin Wall was put up and we played in the stadium where the 1936 Olympics had taken place. I return in 1962, by which time the wall had been erected and there were lots of movement restrictions in place. With what little spare time I had I either played

Military Service

hockey or went rock climbing and, in 1963, I also managed a holiday skiing in Austria. We were not encouraged to go out and mix with the local residents. Instead, we were allowed to build a club room in the attic of the accommodation block, which included a bar and games room. One of the crazes that had started up while I was in Germany was go-karting. Not the modern ones you see today, but made-up frames with converted lawnmower engines. I was not too keen on driving them, but I enjoyed making them.

At work I was getting involved with the maintenance and repair of missile equipment, the main purpose of the regiment. There was a large detachment of American soldiers attached to the missile regiment who controlled the war heads of the Corporal Missile, a 60 foot one which had been developed from an old V2 rocket from the last war but with a nuclear war head. We tried on many occasions to mix with them, but they kept themselves to themselves.

During these first few years I concentrated on improving my trade qualifications and, within four years, I became a Lance-Corporal and an A1 tradesman. After four years with the missile regiment, I was posted on an emergency tour to Borneo to be based in Kuching. This posting was meant for my rock-climbing friend, but he did not want to go because he was due to get married in a few months. So, after a few phone calls, I got the posting.

On the island of Borneo, the Indonesians were coming across the border into Sarawak and claiming it as their country and so there was a war going on. We helped the

Military Service

Malaysian forces defend Sarawak. This was 1964, and the crisis had been going on for about two years, so the army was well established out there. My main duties were to support the Gurkha Regiments, going to their locations along the border to repair their equipment as and when required. It was a job I thoroughly enjoyed. This is what I had been trained for. There was a big difference between being in Kuching and being at the border. In Kuching we lived on a swamp in wooden huts with grass roofs, whereas up country we lived in tents in clearings in the jungle close to small villages. Now days I look at the holiday brochures for Borneo, Sarawak and Brunei and the places around there now and it is completely different from when I was there. There were few roads out of Kuching, just tracks. We travelled up rivers by boat or flew, mainly by helicopter, to the various small villages around the country. Sometimes I was flown up to the border locations as a priority to do urgent repairs. My return would often take some time because I was no longer a priority. The people there were amazing. The Dayaks and Rungus, who were the natives of the country, lived in long houses. They had wonderful arrays of ornaments and, to me, strange customs which I got to learn about and enjoyed. Woodcarving and tool making, building long houses, often 100 meters or more in length. They also made clothing from disused parachutes used for dropping supplies along the borders.

I managed to play hockey on the few occasions and most nights after work played volleyball against the Gurkhas.

Military Service

About halfway through my tour the REME staff were relocated to some part-built local commercial shops up the road from the main camp with no perimeter fence. We still had to take our meals in the main camp and do our guard duties there. The building had no windows or doors and all we had to sleep on was our camp beds. During one weekend off, four of us went down the river and climbed Mount Santubong. It was not a very high mountain, but it was jungle all the way to the top and it took us all day and a night to complete the climb.

For most of the time I was out there, I employed a dhobi waller, a local who did the soldiers washing in return for payment. During the football season in the UK, I would post off his football pools coupons via the military postal service. He told me local mail would take weeks, and in return he did my washing first and for less money than the other men. In 1965, after a year out there, I was posted back to Germany. I asked to stay in Borneo, but they would not let me because of my knowledge of missile handling equipment I was required back at the missile regiment where I had been before. However, they owed me a month's leave, which I took in Singapore on my way back to the UK. An enjoyable time off with lots of swimming and, of course, the occasional beer.

Back to Dortmund in Germany where I carried on the same old role with the missile handling equipment. I had often though about joining the Parachute Regiment, but when

Military Service

applying I was told I was needed in my current role. I spent a lot of my time living under canvas, travelling around all parts of Germany, repairing equipment and being part of the NATO force that was defending Western Europe in the Cold War of the 1960s. Every year the regiment was required to go to the Outer Hebrides to test-fire the missiles. During the last year I was with them I went to Benbecula, which was part of the Outer Hebrides. I worked there for a month taking vehicles out of mothballs and getting them ready for the regiment to come up and fire the missiles. They were fired from North Uist and went out into the North Atlantic and were monitored from a little island called St Kilda. On completion of this assignment, and because the equipment was not going to be used up there again, we had to bring it back by landing craft from the Outer Hebrides, via Lands' End, to Antwerp and then drive it down to Dortmund. On passing down the Irish Sea, we were caught by a force ten gale for about two days. The ship was a flat bottom landing craft it was not a pleasant experience for someone who gets sea-sick having a bath!

My last duty for the regiment was to go back to England and take part in the celebrations for the 250th anniversary of the Royal Artillery on Horse Guards Parade. We were stopped by the Prime Minister's Secretary because the noise we were making was interrupting talks with the French Foreign Minister. As the regiment was disposing of its equipment, I was then posted to the Brigade Headquarters to run a small workshop maintaining the vehicles and equipment they used. During this short stay I was promoted to full corporal.

In 1967, I was posted to Maralinga on the Nerada Plains in South Australia. This was the site used in the 1950s for testing rockets and atomic bombs. I went as part of a group to permanently close the ranges. This was planned to take six months at the most. We filled in all the holes and buried the equipment that had been used in the tests. The ranges, which were the size of Ireland, were to be handed back to the Aborigines who had been trying to get the land back for years as it was part of their ancient territory.

During my time there I travelled around a lot in the desert which was quite enjoyable. There were no real roads, only track marks from previous vehicles. On one of these occasions, I was travelling in a Land Rover with another guy heading to a place called Emu when he turned the Land Rover over. The sun had been shining in our eyes and, in the desert, you went up and down small sand dunes, into craters and sometimes there were bushes and trees on the track. On this occasion there was a tree right in front of us; he swerved to avoid it and rolled the vehicle over onto its roof. Neither of us was hurt but our radio was broken so we could not call for assistance. Thinking we were only a short distance away, maybe an hour's walk from Emu, we started off on foot along the track. It was getting dark, but we thought, as we were so close, it was worth a walk. After about an hour we realised we were not getting anywhere. We were not where we thought we were, and we would have to return to the vehicle. When we got back it was quite dark. Because of the way the Land Rover was lying on a slope I thought that we could use the jack and props to get the vehicle back onto its wheels, which we did. It took us all night and it was hard work, but we succeeded. With a few adjustments to the vehicle's engine, we managed to get it going and then studied our map and decided to re-trace our route from the day before to find out where we were. We managed to find our bearings and arrived at Emu the following morning. Nobody had realised we were missing so they had never bothered to look for us.

Most days when I was in the main camp, I managed to play badminton. On completion of our work on the ranges there was a holdup on a leaving date, so we were given permission to take leave over Christmas 1967. Four of us went up the Murray River and learnt water-skiing and horse riding. On return, and after a lot of negotiations between the Australian and the British Governments, the range was finally handed back to the Aborigines. Due to the hold-ups, I had been out here for nearly a year.

So back to Germany again. This posting was to a large workshop in Minden. I cannot say I enjoyed my stay; I was the senior NCO living-in, which meant if there were any problems, I was called for. Unless I went out the barracks it felt like I was on duty 24 hours a day. This was early 1968 and I only had a few months left to serve for the completion

Military Service

of my three years boy service and nine-year regular service. During this short time, I spent three months in the south of France supporting a tank regiment workshop. I even got to drive the occasional tank.

On return, and because of my interest in rock climbing and canoeing, I was offered a posting to Kristiansand in Norway. This was a Royal Marine outward-bound establishment for climbing and snow training. I was required to repair the vehicles which were used to ferry supplies backwards and forwards from Germany. When not doing so I would assist the instructors on the various courses. There was one problem; I only had a few months left to serve and the Army wanted me to sign on for another three years to get the posting. I had heard about people signing on and not getting the posting they had applied for. So, I decided to call it a day and leave the Army altogether. I returned to the UK in July, took a short course in welding at the Army Resettlement Centre, before finally reporting to the REME depot to hand in my kit, sign some forms and walk out the gates. At the gate, I was stopped and sent back to the main office. They had forgotten to present me with my Campaign Service Medal for Borneo. I completed my service in August 1968 and never heard from the army again, a sad end to an enjoyable part of my working life.

Early Days - Boys Service

My Bedroom in Sarawak, 1964

Rock Climbing

A trip down river to climb Mount Santubong

Passage to Maralinga 1967 Style - Gordon Culpin.

During March 1967 a team of REME and RE personnel went out to Maralinga for six months to clean up the ranges and make ready for a hand over. British Eagle Airways flew us out from London. Stopping at Singapore overnight (Old Raffles Hotel) and flying on the next day via Darwin for customs clearance direct to Maralinga Airfield. I could go on about the many interesting happenings during my stay but will save it until the next reunion. After six months and a lot of hard work the job was done, so most of the Maralinga staff, both military and civilians, left. However a few, including myself, stayed for the hand over.

The months went by during which time contractors came and with our help dismantled the powerhouse and transported the scrap to Watson for an unknown destination. At the same time an American flying club got permission to purchase the Mustangs left at the old test site, and after a short time three where flown out and the others transported out by road.

Just before Christmas '67 we were given leave on the condition we return to Maralinga, should the hand over not take place. Had a wonderful time caravanning up the Murray River. In early January '68 we were informed the hand over had taken place and the Australian Army would be using it as a training camp. So, on completion of our leave we returned to the U.K.

Above: View of Maralinga Village.

Oil Exploration

Within in a month of leaving the army I had obtained employment with a company called Seismograph Service Limited, SSL for short. They worked carrying out oil exploration all around the world. In 1969 my first posting was to Cameroon in West Africa. To prepare me for working on boats, I attended a fibre glass course and an outboard motor course. I flew out via Paris and Lagos, arriving late in the day in East Cameroon. This was the French speaking part of the country and, as I did not speak French, I had difficulty in making myself understood. Nobody turned up to meet me, and so I had to find my own way around. Nobody had heard of SSL, so I took a taxi into town, requesting to be taken to the British Embassy or equivalent. I arrived at the British Bank of West Africa and was told by the driver that the manager was the British representative in the country. He arranged for me to be taken to a flat that SSL hired when they were in town, explaining that they might not return for some days as they had only just left. After two days a member of the crew arrived and said he had just picked up the telegram to say I was coming. I was to join the crew on an island off the coast in two days' time, about an hour's boat ride away. This island of Manoka had a French managed sawmill with a small village attached. All their sawing equipment was driven by steam, the fuel coming from the offcuts of wood. The small village on the island was built on stilts with wooden walkways between the huts, one of which was the local shop and bar. Once a week we took our local workers to the bar for a drinks night.

My role was as a mechanic was repairing boats and equipment used by the crew. We set up camps alongside rivers as a base for the survey crew. Here we lived in tents, propped up on stilts, on riverbanks all along the coast of Cameroon. These were very similar to the conditions that I had experienced in Borneo. I enjoyed this environment, although it rained nearly every day. Toilets were always a problem, but we overcame this by building a landing stage out to the low tide marker with a small cabin on the end. The toilet was flushed twice a day when the tide came in. I mixed a lot with the locals and did quite a bit of work repair to their equipment, pots and pans and various other things in the villages. It was hard but enjoyable work and I had to work months at a time without a day off. I only managed to get to the main city on one occasion. That required a six-hour boat ride and eight hours by track and road. Once was enough! During my time there I made a set of water skis and, much to the amazement of the locals, I skied round the local fishing boats returning into the bay.

As part of the surveying work explosives were used as a way of putting energy into the ground and then recording the returning shock waves were recorded and analysed the results to establish what the subsoil was made up of. This has the side effect of stunning or killing fish in the surrounding water that then floated to the surface. The locals wanted to collect the fish as it was much easier that fishing, but it was dangerous for them to be close to where we were surveying. To keep them safe and maintain their goodwill, we let off some explosives out at sea once a month to increase their fishing catch. Unfortunately, they began to think that it was their right and when on one occasion we forgot, they stormed the beach, surrounded me and demanded more fish. As I was the only member of the crew around at the time, I could not help but I told them I would arrange more explosives soon and fortunately they were happy.

Most of the time during my stay was spent in the West Cameroon, the English-speaking part. There was a Cameroon naval ship guarding us while we worked as we were located close to the Nigerian border where there was a war going on. The government felt we may be in danger from deserters and refugees coming across the border and attacking us. Apart from a few dead bodies on the beach we had no contact with the war. During my spare time I had built a British style drinks bar, complete with hanging wine glasses, a polished bar top and even a foot rail made from a launch drive shaft. Some evenings I would invite some of the naval crew to the bar for drinks. I would go out to their ship moored half a mile out into the bay, pick them up, and return them after drinks. A good time was had by all. One day an officer asked if some of his crew could do some rifle practice on the beach. I set up a small range, using a fallen tree and some beer cans, which they missed most of the time. When asked if I would like to have a go, I hit them all; they did not know I had been a marksman in the army.

I was having an interesting stay, but I was suffering from severe ulcers on my legs due to having to wading in water half the time and these never healed. So, I decided to apply for another post and returned to the UK awaiting transfer to Oman. While I was waiting, I joined a crew doing a survey along the south coast of England. All the way along the A27 from Fareham to Hastings, taking us three months.

Oman was a totally different environment to The Cameroons. I would be out in the desert approximately 500 miles from the nearest road. In early 1970 I flew to Dubai from Stansted Airport on a transport plane sitting on top of the cargo. We arrived twelve hours later at an airfield called Azaba near Muscat. The heavy trucks had been brought out by sea and had to be off-loaded on to barges to be taken into the docks, which were very shallow. After a couple of days checking the vehicles and repairing some of them, we set out from Muscat to drive the 500 miles out into the desert to set up the survey team camp. To get there we had to drive up to the mountains, which ran round the back of Muscat, through gaps in the mountains and out onto the wadis and plains of Oman. There was miles and miles of nothing, no roads, just tracks going off into different directions where oil surveying teams had been working. It took us nearly three days of hard

Oil Exploration

work, getting bogged in and digging ourselves out, but finally got to a location way down into Dhofar, the southern state of Oman, and right on the Yemen border. On arrival we had to set up camp and get the generators up and running. We had caravans with air-conditioning, so some of us were able to live in quite luxurious accommodation compared with our labourers. They lived in tents which were always put well away from the main camp because the Bedouin people were not very hygienic. They were clean enough in their own tents, but they would walk a hundred yards to do their business and then come back very quickly, as there was many flies. If they were anywhere near our camp, the files would continue to be around them and us as well.

Water was always a problem. We had a drilling rig that was used to drill for water, but it was not easy to find. The water had to be tested to make sure it was fit for consumption. Quite often we had to drink it before testing, boiling it first, because the previous source had run out. Sometimes the results came back as unfit for camels to drink but did not seem to bother us that much. I was required to work three months on and one month off. After three months I would be flown out and I could have four weeks leave in the UK or a ticket on a plane to the equivalent cost of going back to the UK. So, I went skiing in the winter, and enjoyed sun and sand in the summer. Most times I went back to the UK and onto on a holiday that I had booked when on a previous holiday break. Once, when I returned to Oman, I took carrot seeds and fertiliser and at customs check they first thought it was drugs but, when I explained, they let me in. I manage to grow them with a lot of tender care.

As you can imagine it was extremely hot, reaching fifty degrees centigrade in the height of the hot season. The local Bedouin people would not work during the midday sun but, like the old song goes, the Englishman goes out in the midday sun, and we carried on working. They got under the trucks, or any shade they could find, and rested for a couple of hours. We got up around six in the morning and worked for a couple of hours, had breakfast, then went back to work. We usually continued until late in the evening and would do a good twelve to fourteen hours per day, seven days a week, for three months, so we earned our month off. When Christmas came, we were unaware and did not have a celebration, just carrying on our normal work routine. Every few months we would move our main camp closer to where the daily surveying was taking place. Once it was more than one hour's ride each way, we moved. At one stage I was asked to build a runway for a DC3 aircraft to land because we had moved so far away from the nearest one. With the aid of a truck, we dragged several barrels full of sand placed on a platform to level out a suitable runway. The first aeroplane landed a week later with no problems.

We were in an area of Oman which was a couple of hundred miles inland where few people lived. We had to recruit our labourers from further north. They worked for about six weeks and then they took a truck with a crowd of them on the back to where they used to live, for a couple of weeks break. As their tribes were nomadic and always moving from one wadi to another, they had to try and find out where their families had gone to. A wadi was often several hundred miles long by a hundred miles wide so they would take some time to find out where their families were. They would stay for a couple of weeks and then they would come back. We always had enough surplus crew members to allow for this. Bearing in mind there are no roads or maps of this area other than the barren desert, these guys would always be able to find their way there and then their way back. If the vehicle they were driving broke down, they usually managed to fix it with string and wire somehow. On one occasion I went out looking for them, because they were overdue. I found them broken down, fixed their vehicle, and got them back on their way. I also got to know my way around.

I remember returning to Oman from one leave during Ramadan. The two guys that used to drive the tankers up to the coast for fuel and bring it back down to us were observing their holy month. They said that they would not come back during Ramadan because they would be too tired as they could not eat during the daytime. As they were running out of fuel at the site five hundred miles to the southwest, they asked me to drive one of these trucks. A ten-thousand-gallon articulated truck through the desert! I got some water and food and off I went, through the mountains and up on to the plateau. When I got up there, there were no signposts to show me the way and I was not quite sure which direction to go. There was some local Bedouin tribesman sitting

Oil Exploration

round a fire, and I asked them if any of them spoke English. They looked at me a bit strangely, so I kept saying, "Haima, Haima", and they said, "yeah, yeah", and pointed in a certain direction. So off I went. After sixteen hours driving, and a lot of digging, I arrived at a place called Haima. One hut and a tent. It was late at night and all I could see was a light in the distance. I had had enough driving, so I parked up and went to sleep in the truck. In the morning I woke and saw some tents about half a mile away, so I went across to the tents to see who they were. It was one of our other crews who were on the move and had been pitched there for a few days. One of the members of my crew, another mechanic, had driven up in his Land Rover from our camp to meet me and assist me to get back. We shared the driving, and it took us almost three days to get to base camp, often having to dig ourselves out because there were no roads. For miles there were only sand dunes, wadis and, after a shamal (sandstorm), there were just huge piles of sand, six, eight, ten feet high. The tracks would disappear into a sand dune where four or five hours before, it would have been just flat.

Life was not easy, but I enjoyed it. I found a gazelle on the roadside as I was coming back from one location. Its mother had been killed so I took it in hand and kept it on the camp site and I had some wonderful times with it. If I wanted to get its attention, I only had to shake a cornflakes box and it was there in seconds. Sometimes when I was working around the workshops it would come up to play and I used to run round a Land Rover and, when it was chasing me, I would jump on the back of the vehicle. The gazelle would take some time for it to realise where I was. This was the nearest I got to taking part in sport while in Oman. After a few months the gazelle disappeared for a few days, returning looking the worse for wear. A month later it was gone, most likely looking for another gazelle to breed with.

Many tribesmen we employed were strange people, but I got on with them alright, even without being able to speak the language. They could not speak English but sign language and body language tells a lot and I'm quite a funny sort of guy so I can act the fool and they would enjoy that and take on board what I was trying to pass over to them. Quite often I would be asked to repair equipment for them such as rifles or jewellery. When they had saved some money and bought more jewellery, they would ask me to attach to their wife's existing jewellery. The wife would walk around with jewellery hanging down from her ears, around her waist and down her chest and this was a sign of prosperity within the tribe. Some of the old weapons I had repaired were homemade and had no rifling in the barrel. They made their own cartridges which were huge, at least two inches. After I had repaired one, they would say, "Do you want to fire the first shot?", and I said, "no, you can do that". I was never sure that it would not blow up in my face. Sometimes they would bring silver charms and things and want me to fix to the side of the rifle. Again, it was more of an adornment to their status rather than a weapon of war. On occasions, I

Oil Exploration

got to unpack a brand new 7.62 rifle like I had used in the army, which they had bought on the coast and wanted me to degrease and test it for them. Despite all the weapons, I never got threatened and I never felt unsafe with these guys.

I remember one time I was doing some work on a truck, and I stuck a crowbar in my leg causing an injury. We had a nurse on the crew, an Indian nurse, but he only did minor repairs. It was quite a nasty gash in my thigh, and it needed stitching up but he said that this was a minor repair to him. The Bedoo people sat round and watched as I had my leg stitched up without any anaesthetic and they were amazed that I did not cry or scream out. As a result, I became quite a hero. When they had any illnesses, the nurse used to give them tablets, but they used to throw them away and say the only way you can cure an illness is by pain, and they wanted pain like Mr Culpin had had.

There was a war going on out in Oman at the time that I was out there. It was away on the coast, round the town of Salalah, the other side of a big mountain range between us and the coast. We did occasionally get insurgents from the Yemen coming through and they would demand water and fuel from us. There would usually be twenty or thirty of them with rifles and bandoliers, driving old vehicles left over from the last war. We were told by the government just give them what they wanted, and they would probably go away, which they did. Both times I was the only white man in the camp; the rest were away doing their seismic surveying. People have asked me if I was frightened by them, but I just

Oil Exploration

took it in my stride. I did not think they were any real threat to me unless I refused them the fuel and water they wanted. Many years later I read a book about the war in Oman. The author of the book suggested that over the mountains from where the war was, there was a no-man's land. He said it was uninhabitable and no one could, or did, live there. Unknown to him I was working there at the time. I did write to the editor of the book to let him know that I had been out there during this time, but I never got a reply.

In early 1971, after about a year and a half of working three months on and one month off, I started to review my life. Although I enjoyed the work I was doing, I could see myself just becoming a nomad, working in a desert for the rest of my life or till I was not fit enough to do so. The firm was quite happy with my work, more than happy on most occasions, but did I want to do this for the rest of my life? I finally concluded that I was at a time in my life that I should change, perhaps try and settle down and have a family and become a normal sort of person. So, after working a three-month notice period, I returned to England to decide what I was going to do from then on.

Shallow Marine Seismic Surveys

PARTY-440

45 ft. RECORDING CATAMARAN
CAMEROUNS '69
Seismograph Service Limited

Oil Exploration, 1969

⛓ Between Jobs ⛓

I arrived back in England in mid-1971. In a very short time, I got a job at Caffyns, a local garage, just to see me over till I decided what I was going to do. This was a mundane job, I did not do any overtime and working on cars gave you poor pay. I had rented a small studio cottage on the seafront at Sandgate near Folkestone, because I did not really want to live with my parents. I needed the freedom to do whatever I wanted, when I wanted to do it. In those days, as a single man, some things were not easy to do, such as opening a bank account. I had been out of the country for almost three years, banking in the Bahamas and having my money transferred across to a bank in Jersey. Whenever I came to England I would nip across to Jersey and take some money out, as I was a non-taxpayer and a non-resident. I had always paid my national insurance stamp, but to open a bank account in those days you needed up-to-date references, which I did not have. I already had an overseas account with Barclays, but the local manager would not accept that as sufficient. Eventually, my father persuaded him to let me open an account with Barclays in Folkestone and I was able to transfer my money from Jersey to the UK. I was advised by somebody who had come back from overseas to go to the

Income Tax Office and declare whatever money I brought into the country and pay some tax on it and then I would not have any problems when I got a job. This is what I did, and I paid around £50, which was quite a bit in those days, but I could well afford it.

While working at Caffyn's I bought my first car. Although I was 31, I had never owned a car because I had not been in the country long enough to warrant it. I bought a Morris Oxford which was a bit old, but I quite liked it. It was a stable steady car. I joined the local hockey club and played regularly with them during the season and travelled all over Kent playing away games. I also joined the Folkestone Hythe Lions Club which was quite a pleasant gathering of people; and we did work for the general public on community and voluntary work. We set up a Donkey Derby every year and a pram race down on the seafront, stopping at all the pubs on the way.

In early 1972, I met my future wife, Wendy. I thought I needed a better car - to keep up with the Jones', so to speak. So, I bought a flash orange Ford Capri V4 which had an aerial and a black roof and a great big, long bonnet on it. I had thoughts at that time of becoming a driving instructor because I was quite a patient, careful driver, and thought my skills might allow me to set up my own business. So, I took an Advanced Driving test to see whether I was up to standard or not. Most people had to do some training for it, but I signed up to it and took my test in Tunbridge Wells. The tester said only one thing let me down, I did not use my

Between Jobs

horn on country roads, but I got a pass. I became a member of the Institute of Advanced Motorists thinking it would be an advantage in life. I was told by the instructor that, if I mentioned my membership when I applied for insurance on my car, I would get it a lot cheaper. I did this and found that it was twice as expensive as I was already paying.

The rented cottage on the seafront in Sandgate, was costing me more money for rent per week than I was getting paid as a mechanic in the workshop. I was eating into my savings and so I had to quickly look around for a better paid job. I saw a job advertised for a firm called Contiki. The company ran tours all round Europe, taking people camping, particularly females from Australia and America who were on their own and who wanted to explore Europe. They wanted me to set up a workshop base in Folkestone and service the transit vehicles when they came back, making them ready for the next tour. They would go out for up to nine weeks and spread out as far as Moscow, Istanbul and Morocco. Contiki was based in London, and to encourage people to join the overseas trips they laid on pub trips around central London. I was invited, free of charge, which I took up many times. A good evening was had by all.

This job also entailed going abroad occasionally. I remember going to Liechtenstein to repair a vehicle that needed the engine rebuilding because of a fault in the timing belts. I set off at midnight and got there later the next day. This transit was on its way to the Munich Olympic Games and, as the campers had tickets for the games, they hoped I could fix it. I worked all night and managed to rebuild the engine and get it back on the road so they could get away. The owner of the garage where I was doing the repairs stood watching for a long time and when I had finished, he offered me a job, saying he had never seen a mechanic work like me. While I was there, I was told about another breakdown which was in Heidelberg. It was in a Ford garage, who had stripped the engine down but had no spare parts. I had not got any spare parts either, and so, I had to tow this transit van all the way back to England via Luxembourg, rebuild the engine and get it ready for the start of its next trip the following day.

I was courting Wendy at the time but as I was still single and so I could work all sorts of odd hours. Some tour buses used to come back in the middle of the night and, as they were going to go back out again that day, I would have to service them through the night and have them ready for the tour the next morning. The firm Contiki finally decided to move their base to Belgium where they could use bigger coaches and make more money with people coming across the channel as foot passengers. They offered me a job there, but I did not want to move there because I was courting Wendy.

As I have said, it was not difficult then to get a job as a mechanic. They were crying out for people who had the range of experience I had. A firm called Intercity Trucks were operating from Lympne Airport, near Folkestone. They initially wanted somebody to rebuild a truck which had crashed in Europe. They could not get new trucks because there was an eighteen-month waiting list, but they could get the parts if somebody could rebuild one. I spent about six months in total, rebuilding this truck with all new parts, chassis, engine, cab and all the associated parts that go with it. By the time I left the firm that truck had done 100,000 miles, so I reckon I did not do a bad job! Shortly after starting with this company, I bought a house. At the time, as a bachelor, this was very difficult to do and getting a mortgage was almost impossible. The banks did not lend money for mortgages and building societies would only lend to families. However, I managed it and when we got married, we moved into a hundred-year-old terraced house. The first of nine houses we were to live in.

Intercity Trucks asked me to go with an escort vehicle to Rome to retrieve part of an aeroplane which had crashed and bring it back to England on a big low-loader. Going out there and complying with different road laws took over a month because the vehicle needed special permission to travel on certain roads at certain times of the day. I remember getting jammed under a bridge in Nice and they had to stop the railway line for three hours while they checked and confirmed that there was no structural damage. On arriving at Rome airport, I had to help build a platform for a section of the plane to be mounted on. It still overlapped the truck either side but was high enough to miss parked cars. The load measured 13'6" wide and 60' long. Because of a fuel shortage, due to problems in the Middle East, we discovered there was a restriction on trucks travelling in Italy at the weekend, so we had to hold up for a couple of days at Pisa Airport. On the way through Southern France, we got as far as Marseille and decided that we would have a rest, as most of the time we were sleeping in the vehicles. We left the main vehicle there and drove one of the cars back to England just for a weekend, after which it took us another week or so to get back to Folkestone.

Intercity Trucks were based at Lympne Airport but there was talk about closing it down and moving the workshops further afield, something I did not want to do, so I started looking around again for another job.

My brother said to me, "Why do not you come out and work in the North Sea oil fields?". By this time he had left the Royal Navy and he was a deep-sea diver working on the North Sea and earning fabulous money. He said, "You can get good money out there so why don't you come out there and give it a try?". I spoke to Wendy and, although she was not too keen on me being away from home, she always allowed me to carry on doing the things I wanted to do and so I applied for the job and got it. I thought I was only going to work week on, week off, but they said, due to my lack of experience of working on an oil rig, they wanted to see me working as a boiler man or motorman on board first for a year. If I was successful, I could carry on as a mechanic.

Mechanics worked one week on and one week off, but a boiler man worked two weeks on and two weeks off. If I had known this, I would never have taken the job.

Out on the rigs in bad weather the waves could reach more than 60 feet. Each Monday an evacuation drill would be held, where we all had to report to a boat station. Each life raft held 14 personnel, but often there would be more than 20 waiting to get on. The drill involved the life raft bring thrown over the side of the rig and we would have to jump into the sea, some 80 foot below, as if it was the real thing. Thank God we never had to do it for real!

It was hard work. We worked twelve hours on and twelve hours off and I soon realised that this was not what I wanted to do. I was missing my family and I wanted to get back home and be with my wife. It was not just working on the oil rigs, but it was also the getting there and getting back; you never knew what the weather was going to be like. Sometimes you could get an aeroplane from Norwich to Esbjerg, in Denmark, and then fly out by helicopter. Other times I would have to go by boat and then wait for weather changes. The first time I could not get off for three weeks; so, it was not very good for family life. There were 12-hour shifts with no breaks, and I had to put up with the Tool Pusher, the head man on the rig. When drilling was being carried out, he would shout at me down the speaker system saying, *"nigger give me some more steam"*, or some other demand. He came from Texas, where a lot talked to non-whites like that and, despite being white myself, he still spoke to me

Between Jobs

that way. My opposite number was an American called Bill and the Tool Pusher called him Bill. I was not happy and told him so. Some days I would have to go down one of the rig legs to check the oil in the sea water pumps. Not a nice job in bad weather, when that meant going down the inside of a leg when the sea waves could be 60 feet high. Another job I had was to refuel the helicopters, sometimes when the rotors were still going! This was not the life for Wendy and me, so, I gave in my notice and left.

In 1975 I was back working in Folkestone for the Department of Environment. This job required me to go round repairing vehicles for different government departments including prisons. When I was not going out, I was rebuilding Land Rovers. All the Land Rovers from different ministries, when they had seen their time out or were beyond repair, would come to Folkestone. I had to build perhaps one good Land Rover out of three old ones. These reclaimed Land Rovers were then sent to disaster areas all over the world. The workshops were trade union led and they kept insisting that I had to join the union, because they were a hundred percent unionised, and I was the only non-member. Being the stubborn sort of person I was, I said, "No, I am quite happy as I am". They told me that they could make it difficult for me if I did not join and so I said, "Well, I'll tell you what. I'll join if every member of your union branch does a decent day's work, turns up five days a week, and works on the vehicles and not on private jobs. Then I will join the union, until that time I won't". I never heard any more about it. One of the most interesting jobs I did was to overhaul a large V12 engine mounted in a dredging barge moored in Chatham docks yards. I was chosen because of the experience I had with large engines. It was a week's hard work including travelling to and from each day. I took an apprentice mechanic with me who gained a lot of experience that he would never have got in the main workshops.

There had been talk for some time about this workshop closing due to government cutbacks, so again, I started looking at what I was going to do with my future? It was now 1977. We had been married since April 1973; we had had one child and we had moved home from the old bachelor house to a modern bungalow. It only had two bedrooms and we were thinking of expanding our family so we would need to move. I had responsibilities now and I had to settle down. Did I want to remain a mechanic for the rest of my life? I had noticed that older mechanics suffered badly from arthritis and other joint pains due to crawling around on cold hard floors. This could be me in a few years' time. I needed to change direction.

Although I was always up for a challenge, I needed to have a secure job for the future with a pension at the end of it. During the last two years I had visited many of the prisons in Kent including Dover and Eastchurch. On these visits I had the opportunity to speak to some of the staff and inmates; the staff appeared to have an interesting job. Should I give the prison service consideration? On making enquiries into what qualifications were needed for the prison service, I found out that it was not formal qualifications they were interested in, but more about your life experiences as this was what prison officers needed; experiences in dealing with people from all sorts of backgrounds. This was something I felt I had from my worldwide working experience. So, after talking it through with Wendy, we agreed I should give it a go. I was required to take an exam, which I took and passed. I had a medical and an interview, after which they agreed to employ me. So, in August 1977, I went for a month's trial period at Dover Borstal to see how I would get on and how I liked it. This would be the start of my life behind bars.

The Start of My Life Behind Bars

HM PRISON SERVICE

PURPOSE
VISION
GOALS
VALUES

Her Majesty's Prison Service serves the public by keeping in custody those committed by the courts.

Our duty is to look after them with humanity and help them lead law-abiding and useful lives in custody and after release.

Dover Borstal

I was given an introductory month at Dover before starting my training. Dover Borstal dealt with offenders under 21. A lot of them were as young as 15 or 16, an age which made me feel like an old man. Many of the officers were in their twenties so, at thirty-five, I could have been called 'Dad', which indeed I was in later years. I soon got the feel of what was going on and what a prison officer did and how they behaved on the landing. As a lot of it was interpersonal skills, being able to communicate with different lads from different backgrounds, I felt I had not got a problem. At the end of the month, I was selected to go to the Prison Officer's Training School, which was at Wakefield, for a nine-week training course. I could come home at weekends, so it was not so bad.

The training was not what I expected. I thought there would be a lot more interpersonal skills, but most of it was to do with security; how to search cells, search inmates, apply handcuffs and similar skills which of course we also needed. We did a lot of talking and discussions and there were comments made by observing staff on how we interacted within groups of people, but there did not seem to be a great deal of training to me.

When I had the opportunity to speak in a group, I did. I had a wide good background knowledge, whereas a lot of the other trainee officers were younger and had not done a lot in life. I remember one discussion group talking about what we thought was important when we were considering sending our children to schools. I immediately said that I hoped that my children would be at the standard to go to a grammar school because I thought they gave the best education. The instructor sitting in the background, a principal officer, immediately stood up and said, "You're talking a load of rubbish, there's no such thing as grammar schools anymore". Being the outspoken person, I was, I immediately said, "Well, you haven't lived in Kent or some other counties. They still have grammar schools, and they work very well". He told me I was wrong, but we carried on the discussion. I was later called up in front of the Commandant for answering back to the instructor. I said I was acting as anybody else would have and if somebody told me I was wrong and I knew I was right, I would be obliged to put them in the picture. He said, "There is no such thing as grammar schools". I replied, "There is, and if you want to ring a certain number in Kent, you'll get hold of a grammar school". I made it quite clear that I was not arguing with the instructor, I was just making a point of view which I thought was correct and I thought, in a group, you should be able to do that without anybody condemning you for what you had done. Anyway, nothing came out of it, and I went back to the normal sessions without any problem.

Dover Borstal

We had been told that we could put down in order of priority what postings we would like at the end of the training session and, the week before the end of the course, we would be given the posting. I talked to Wendy about it and asked, "Where would you like to go and live?" She was quite happy to move away from home and, in fact, she thought it was the best thing that could happen. I could put in for a prison in Yorkshire or the Isle of Wight, or anywhere in the country. I put in for a selection away from southeast England but, when the postings were given out, I got Dover Borstal! Apparently, I had made quite a good impression while I was there for the initial month, and they had asked for me when the selection was done. During the last week of training, all the officers going to adult prisons were issued with their uniforms but people working in a borstal did not wear uniforms; they wore smart jackets, shirts and ties. At the end of the course, I had a week's leave then was told to report to Dover Borstal.

Dover Borstal was part of an old Napoleonic era fort, built up on a hillside in Dover. It had a dry moat round it about 20 to 30 feet deep and another moat leading down to the sea where the French prisoners-of-war used to come up. It had been an army barracks in the 1800s with a lot of underground buildings. The inside perimeter was made up of five units capable of holding a total of 300 inmates. There were just over a 100 staff and numerous other civilian instructors, teachers and medical staff.

Dover Borstal

A Borstal sentence in those days was for somebody who was a first-time offender between 15 to 21 years old. They would serve an indeterminate sentence of six months to two years depending on their behaviour. They would have to earn their release. Most went out around the nine-to-twelve-month period but some, who were an exception, went out after six months. All the units had names of the Cinque Ports; the unit I was on was called Hythe House. Hythe House was made up of single rooms and dormitories taking a maximum of 40 trainees at any one time. I quickly realised it had very close similarities to boy service in the army. There was a definite routine and some of the discipline was based on the army methods.

An example of the daily routine would be up at half past six, breakfast, wash, clean, and 'slop out'[1]. The landing officer's job was to make sure they got out of bed, cleaned their kit, and, on certain days, laid it out on the bed, and generally get ready for breakfast and parade. Breakfast was bought to the house from a central kitchen and served in the dining hall. Most of the time there were only two officers on the wing. One would be supervising the breakfast, while the other would be supervising the inmates upstairs and getting them down for breakfast. At about quarter to eight all the inmates

---

[1] The rooms had no internal sanitation. Every inmate had a pot by his bed which he could do his business in and then empty into a large sink on the landing when the door was unlocked.

were paraded outside, fell into three ranks, and marched to a central parade square for a roll call. At 8am the chief officer would take the parade; the rolls would be checked, and then we would march off.

The inmates were grouped into the various work parties and off they would go to their places of work, training areas, education, work parties, or cleaning parties. If they were going back to the unit rather than another part of the prison, they would have to go to the gym for half an hour while the staff, who had started at half past six, went for their breakfast. At about quarter to nine the staff would return, pick up the inmates from the gym, and take them back to their wings for house cleaning. A Senior Officer would oversee the wing and one other officer would be in charge of the cleaning and general duties. I quickly fell into this routine. It was very similar to my early army days and, because they did not know I was a new officer, they just treated me as any other officer, and I was able to get on with my work. I got them working, cleaning the rooms, landings, toilets and whatever else needed to be cleaned around the wing. A high standard was always expected including highly polished floors.

If I was the number three officer on the wing, I would take a group of inmates away for a cleaning or a digging party, or whatever duties they had to do. I spent a lot of time with a group of up to twelve inmates, either on the moat banks, or in the moats cutting grass and generally cleaning round the establishment. If you oversaw a group of inmates,

Dover Borstal

who quite often did not want to be working there, somehow you had to motivate them into getting on with a bit of work and getting through the morning shift and then again in the afternoon. I had quite a few incidents in the early days of inmates refusing to work and demanding to be put in segregation[2] so they did not have to work in the rain. I would not have any of this. I said, "you will stay out here until the work shift ends and if you still do not work, I will place you on report. If you're coming out with me, you're coming out to work and I'll show you how to work".

I used to work alongside the inmates showing them how to cut grass with a scythe or whatever tools we had, and they soon got motivated. If I did the work, they felt they had to do it. I remember one really cold day when we were in the moat and the whole party of ten refused to work. I stood them all along the side wall of the moat, the side where the wind was blowing the hardest, and I stood on the other side where I was out of the wind. I said, "We're going to be here till 12pm. You can work and warm yourselves up and, after a while, I'll get us out of the wind and have a break; but that's what's going to happen. I'm not going to put you down in the cells". A couple relented and, very quickly, they all realised that they were not going to win. After about ten minutes we found a hut to hide in and have a smoke break, but it was very much left up to the officer to get through his shift the best way he could, there was nobody to help you. You did

---

[2] Punishment cells

Dover Borstal

have a radio, but there was nobody going to come to your assistance unless it was an emergency.

At 12.00pm each day the parties and instructional groups would come back inside for their lunch. The changeover of shifts sometimes took place and then at 1.30pm we went back out on parade, had a roll check, and then back out to the working groups. At around about 4.30pm all the parties and work groups were brought back to the wings in preparation for the evening meal. At 5.00pm food was collected from the kitchen and served in the main dining room of each wing and, after they had eaten, they would be locked away so the staff would go for their meal. At 6.00pm all the inmates who were allowed to have association were unlocked and they would come down and take part in various activities within the wing. They could go to the gym for exercise sessions, to education for extra classes, or to the chapel on certain days for religious services. I say "go", but they were all escorted; inmates rarely went around the establishment without an escort. The odd one or two might go down alone to the medical centre if there was no staff available. I would tell them if they went off the road the hidden dogs would get them; they were never sure if I was telling the truth. When there were groups of inmates moving about there were always staff supervising them and marching them to where they were going.

At 8.30pm association would end and all the inmates would go up to their rooms, finish off their ablutions, and then be locked up by 9.00pm ready to handover to the night

Dover Borstal

staff. At 9.00pm the night staff would come on and they would go round and check all the doors were locked and there was the right roll call on each unit. The night staff were called night patrols. Most of them were retired prison officers who were just earning a bit more money after they had left the service at 60. One time, an inmate came to me complaining a night patrol kept switching his cell light on an off during the night and calling him a black 'so and so', and he asked if I could stop him. I told him that, if he did not lay a hand on him, I would forget to lock his cell door that night. When the staff check the doors were locked, they pushed their shoulder against it. As expected, the night patrol went flying into the cell and landed on the inmate's bed. The inmate just lent over him and said, "Now call me a black so and so!". The night patrol looked terrify and said sorry. The inmate thanked me and he had no more problems.

I soon decided that, unless something went wrong, the prison service was the career for me. I was going to make every effort to get promoted and it was my ambition to be a Chief Officer by the time I left at 60. Unfortunately, this was not to be as, a few years later, they did away with Chief Officers, so Principal Officer became my goal.

I quickly realised that the staff came from various outside occupations. Some were very good, but some were very weak in character, and I found it difficult to get on with some of them. I was very grateful for my experience in the army because, when I looked around at some of the

Dover Borstal

other new officers, who had not been in the forces, I saw how difficult it was for them to be on the landing dealing with guys who were a lot bigger than them and a lot more worldly wise. As I had been to Dover before and I knew where everything was, I went straight onto the landing on the induction wing. It was probably the best thing that could happen for me. All new receptions to Dover Borstal were put through the induction wing for a three week period. They were all new to the institution; I was also new, but they did not know it and so I was able to develop my skills in managing them.

Our routine was slightly different to the other wings, providing a three-week induction to borstal life. We would have to explain the whole running of the establishment, and take them to view training areas for courses, such as motor mechanics, plastering, bricklaying, carpentry. We also had to show them how to clean their rooms and lay out their kit for Saturday morning kit inspections. It was very much like being an NCO in the army, which I had done in my service.

In 1978, after I had been there about a year, our son was due to be born and we needed to move house. In those days they had prison officers' quarters and there was a certain number of houses around the prison which were never allowed to be empty. If they were full up, then other officers could claim a housing allowance and 'live out'. I was living out at the time, but one came available, and I had to move in or lose my allowance. So, we sold our bungalow in Folkestone and moved to the Western Heights, right behind the Borstal on top of the hill at Dover. The houses were bleak and sparse, there was no heating apart from a coal stove in the kitchen, but it had beautiful views over Dover towards Dover Castle. Our son was born in November 1978, and it was a really cold winter so, at nights, we used to put him in the airing cupboard in our bedroom, directly above the stove, to keep him warm. During the winter of 1978 I made frames with plastic covering on them to put against the metal windows; not to keep us warm, but to keep the snow out, because the metal windows leaked so much the snow would build up on the inside of the window ledges. You can imagine what it was like in the rest of the house.

We soon got friendly with our next-door neighbours, and we used to help each other out with childcare when necessary. It was not an easy life at the beginning. I worked long hours, and I was away from the family for days on end. I did not see the children other than when I came home or went off in the mornings when they were asleep in bed, but the money was quite good, and we needed it. I found the work very tiring, because you were on the go all day long and, quite often, you were doing 13-hour shifts. Overtime was not voluntary; you were detailed. The only guaranteed time-off was one rest day on a weekend off and one late shift in a week, if you had done more than four late shifts in a row. I could easily work 60 or 70 hours a week, but the extra money was very handy.

Dover Borstal

This job was a whole new challenge to me I had to prove to myself and others that I was up to it. Security, security, security. That took preference over everything I did for the first few years. It was instilled in me from the training I had received. The duty of a prison officer was to maintain the security of the prison, to ensure that everybody was safe, and that the inmates did not escape. Some security procedures are straight-forward and common sense, but others are not so easy to understand until you are in a situation that sometimes you were put in as a prison officer. For example, opening a cell door is not just like opening your front door and walking in. There are certain procedures you need to take before opening the door and during the opening of the door. Who is behind the door? How many are in the cell? Where are they within the cell? Standard cell doors have a small spy hole so you can investigate the cell to see where the inmate is located. If you could not see him, he would be ordered to move away from the doorway or the walls so that you could. You also ensured that he or they, if there was more than one in the cell, would be standing well away from the door so they could not throw it back in your face as you came in. Unlocking the door, you would push it slowly forward, keeping your foot against the door and, once it was partly opened, you would turn the lock of the door again to 'lock it open'[3] and then proceed to push the door forward and go into the cell. There was a

---

[3] By re-locking the door the extended bolt would prevent the door from fully closing.

reason for this. One of the inmates may push the door back at you and if they did so, the door would not lock with you inside. In modern prisons with modern cells, the doors can be opened inwardly or outwardly. This prevented the inmates from barricading the door so you could not get in, which happened to me on a few occasions. You were supposed to carry out this procedure all the time when opening doors, but this was not practical when you had to open sixty cells in a few minutes. You would get to know the inmates and what temperament they were in from handover information on shift changes and only carry this procedure when unsure what was behind the door.

On arriving at the prison, all staff would draw keys. They held a tally; a disc with a number on it, kept on the end of their keychain. They would hand the tally over to the gatekeeper who would give them a set of keys with a corresponding number. These keys would be put on a keychain and were not allowed to be taken off again until they were handed back to the gatekeeper on leaving the prison. When they were not being used, the tallies would be kept in a pouch on the belt, or in the pocket of the person carrying them. Trained prison officers were the only ones who carried the security keys; the ones that opened the wing gates and the cell doors. At Dover there were more dormitories than there were cells, although there were cells for inmates who were removed for various purposes or under punishment. The dormitory doors had quite large windows with glass reinforced with metal.

Dover Borstal

Within a very short time of joining Dover, I could clearly see the similarities between Borstal and boy service in the army. In the army we were not locked up behind bars but there were still very strict rules to follow and severe punishments if you did not adhere to them. One of the advantages of being at Borstal was that almost all the inmates were coming inside for the first time. They may have been in remand homes and perhaps spent a little time on remand waiting to be sentenced, but they had not spent much time in prison. They were coming as new people to an environment they had not experienced so they felt quite intimidated in the first few weeks.

I felt my role as an induction officer was to steady them down and get them used to the rules and regulations so that, when they went on to the main wings, they knew what they had to do and were not shouted at or bullied by others. A lot of the inmates sent to Borstal were not in for very serious crimes. Some had been persistent burglars or had been caught in affrays in the street with other groups of people. It was felt by the courts that a spell in a disciplined environment, where they could be given further education and training and learn what society expected of them, would help them. A lot of the younger ones, 15 or 16-year-olds, were inadequate in society and they needed support and help from the prison staff.

I keep referring to them as inmates, but they were called 'trainees' in the Borstal system. Education was the key thing in getting through to some of these young lads. How were they going to get on in the Borstal? I quickly realised that I had to show them respect and they had to show me respect if we were to get anywhere. We would sit them down in small groups and talk to them about living and existing in prison and getting the most out of it. The most important thing I would say to them was, "Do not waste your time, get a better education, learn some trade skills so that you can perhaps lead a better life when you go outside". I would explain that politeness and respect was not a bad thing, and it could often get you a lot more things in life than you would without it. I would say, "Respect must be earned. You can't just expect it to be there. I am going to earn my respect with you as you have got to do it with me".

A lot of them had come from demanding worlds where they had shouted at people, their parents, their teachers to get what they wanted, and often it worked, so they would carry it on further in their life. I made it clear it did not work with me. Rules were there for a purpose. Without rules in an institution, thing would just become a shambles. I would instil in the trainees that we were not personally getting at them with the individual rules but, to manage a group of trainees, we needed set rules and they had to be adhered to. As I experienced in the army, it did not matter how harsh the regime was, you soon got used to it and, within a few weeks, most of the trainees settled down to this regime and in fact it helped pass to the time.

Unfortunately, with many of the trainees, personal

hygiene and the ability to clean and tidy things was non-existent. We even had bed-wetters who had to be reported and their bedding changed. I remember, if you were near the office about 8.00am, the medical staff came on and would ring up the units one at a time and say, "wets and dries". They would want to know how many people had got wet beds. A lot of the trainees would try to conceal it and hide their sheets all over the place to try and avoid it, or pinch somebody else's. These trainees were registered with the hospital as bedwetters and then the night staff would have to go round and wake the lad up and get him to use the toilet, or the bowl they were all issued with for night use. In later years they developed medication for people who had this problem and it faded out.

During the working part of the day most of the wings were empty of trainees other than a few who were kept on the wings to do the general cleaning. There would also be one or two 'lame and lazy' ones and one or two waiting for probation officer or police interviews. Other than that, there would hopefully be very few on the wings because this was the time when the duty prison staff did their security checks. Locks, bolts and bars had to be checked and signed for daily. Rooms had to be searched at random, or on hearing that there was possibly something concealed. Trainees were only allowed the minimum amount of clothing and personal items and if they had more than that, it was taken away. This made it much easier for searching because you knew what should be there and what should not be there. It may sound easy just to search a room or a cell, but there is quite a lot goes into it and often you would find things in the cell which, though not so obvious, could be a weapon.

In my early years, trainees who shaved would be issued with a razor blade on the landing in the morning for them to have a shave and they had to return it before they went down to breakfast. Within a couple of years, they were being issued with disposable razors, which seemed alright, but these could be converted into knives and all sorts of things. Over time trainees became geniuses in using small things to make a weapon. Biros could look like a biro, but they could be turned into a knife, or the empty sleeve can be used as part of a pipe for smoking cannabis. To give you an example of a weapon; they were allowed portable radios with earphones in their rooms which required batteries. A few batteries in a sock can make quite an effective weapon. To help stop this, they were only allowed the batteries that they had in their set. If they wanted new batteries, they had to hand the old batteries in. We quickly found that most of the weapons the trainees made were not to fight the officers, they were to defend themselves against other bullying inmates. In the late 70s and early 80s drugs were not a problem in prison. The young lads used to sniff glue and such like, but cannabis and heroin were almost unheard of. Trainees could find all sorts of places to hide their ill-gotten gains and it was up to us to try and find them. It was like a game. They would not necessarily hide the things in their cells or in their dormitories, but they would hide them around the buildings, or outside the wings, when they were not using them.

At this time, we had some difficulties in the Borstal because nearly fifty percent, and sometimes over fifty percent, were of West Indian origin whose families had settled in the Brixton area. Although I had experience with people from all ethnic backgrounds, a lot of the staff had not. If you went into Dover town you never saw a person of West Indian origin or, if you did, it was a rarity. To be confronted with fifty percent of them when you were at your work, some staff found very difficult. The West Indians tended to take life inside much easier than the white lads. They accepted doing time as part of life. They committed crimes and, if they got caught once in ten times, then it was bad luck. Quite a lot of them showed no respect for authority and fought the systems all the way; some had a very arrogant and noisy attitude. I did not particularly blame them for the way they behaved because that is how they did it on the outside and they had achieved what they wanted. However, I wanted to show them respect and I expected respect from them so if they came demanding and shouting at me, I just ignored them and pretended they were not even there. When they stopped shouting, I would say, "Is there somebody there who wants to speak to me?". They quickly learnt that shouting at me got them nowhere and we very quickly developed a respect where we could talk on a normal basis. I tried to treat all trainees as individuals. I did not want to know what their crimes were, or what they did or did not do, unless they wanted to tell me. I got my reward when I was working on detached duty at Brixton Prison[4], staying at a hotel up the road. In the evening I would use a phone box across the road, to talk to Wendy. On one occasion a crowd of teenagers came round the box banging on the side. I told Wendy I would have to go expecting a beating when I got outside, but to my surprise, one of the group said, "Hello Mr Culpin, do you remember me? You were my personal offer at Dover". "He was all right", he told the others, and we had a chat about the old days, said goodbye, and went our own ways. I sometimes wonder what would have happened if I had not known this lad!

As for my family life, things had improved slightly because an officer's living quarters had come up in a small village on the outskirts of Dover. A senior officer had retired from the prison service and his house became vacant and was put up for reallocation. I thought that I would never get it as a junior officer, but I applied and got it. This was a modern semi-detached house with central heating, double glazing, a garage, and was very close to a big park. Oh, to be warm in the winter!

For the first few years I worked most of my regular shifts on the induction unit but most of my overtime was worked

---

[4] Occasionally officers were sent to other prisons to make up shortfalls in staff, this was known as Detached Duty.

Dover Borstal

on other units or other jobs within the prison or outside the prison. One of the jobs I used to get regularly was as an escort to magistrates and crown courts. Most of them were in London because our main catchment area for trainees was from the London area. If they had further charges, they would be going to courts in London. Most of the escorts were done on your rest days. It meant an early start of about six o'clock in the morning and not returning to the prison until seven, eight or sometimes nine o'clock at night. In those days we wore civilian clothes, and we would be transported by a local taxi contractor. There were two officers, one of them handcuffed to the trainee being taken to court. At one of the London magistrates' courts, I was pushed into a cell, hand cuffed to the inmate, and the door locked. When I banged on the door to be let out, he said, "shut up, you're not due in court for another two hours". He did not realise I was a prison officer. Good old Met police!

On arrival at a crown court, after handing our prisoner over to the cell staff, we would be logged in and become part of the staff manning the courts. That usually meant spending long hours sitting as a dock officer listening to cases which had already been running for days, but you only ever heard one day of the whole case. Often that is why we were there, just a shortage of staff, the trainee we had escorted were just on the reserve list and was never called up. At a magistrate's court we would hand over to the police. They ran the jail, as they called them, and they would lock up all the trainees and we would just stand by observing what was going on. One of the biggest problems was that many of the magistrate's courts were not very secure because they were very old buildings and parts of town halls or similar places. We had to be very careful that we did not interfere with the police, but still kept control over the security of the inmate.

I have been to the Old Bailey numerous times and sat in on some quite high-profile cases, but when you only saw one or maybe two days of what was going on the case did not make a lot of sense. Another escort duty that we did was transferring prisoners from one prison to another. They would either being transferred permanently or going for a temporary period. Sometimes I would go to one of the allocation units in London and pick up the new allocations for Dover and bring them back. That was quite often done by coach because there could be twenty or thirty at a time. I remember one allocation run where the coach we were in was involved in an accident with a truck. The coach ended up on the barrier of the central reservation of the A2 with the trailer of the truck smashed against the doors of the coach. I was in charge of the escort at the time, and I had twenty trainees who all suddenly wanted to go to the toilet. There was a small toilet across the road in a lay-by, but we could not get out of the main doors. The only way I could get them to a toilet was out the back emergency window above the back seats. This was done, two at a time, handcuffed, and then taken across the main road into the toilet.

I remember going to Chichester Crown Court one time and we had set off at 5.30am for a 10am appearance. The roads were so busy, particularly through Brighton, so that we got there about ten minutes after the opening of the court. I was called into the court to speak to the judge and explain why we were late. He was not a very tolerant sort of person and would not accept my explanation, so I said, "Well, the only way we could have got here on time was to drive over the vehicles in front of us". We had done our best, but he was not very happy although he accepted it in the end. On another escort the taxi we were in broke down with a flat battery and needed a push start. So, there was me outside the door, handcuffed to a trainee who was sitting on the seat, pushing the taxi to get it started. I think my longest escort was transporting a trainee all the way to Manchester. While we were on the M1 motorway, the lad wanted to use the toilet, so we pulled into a busy motorway station and I took him, handcuffed, across to the toilets and back. While we were sitting there having a rest, a van pulled up alongside us and a man came out with some brand-new duvets and covers and asked us if we wanted to buy them. He did not realise this was a prison escort because we were in civilian clothes, and he could not see me handcuffed to the inmate. I told him to go away but he would not take any notice. He said, "I'm not talking to you, I'm talking to the other person there." So, I raised the handcuffs above the seat, he took one look at them, and ran back into the van and was gone!

Working parties were where you had to use your management skills. You would often have up to ten or twelve trainees working on various type of jobs, such as clearing up rubbish, cleaning gardens or scrubbing floors. There was also work outside the prison grounds in all weathers and it was up to you to keep them occupied. Most of the trainees on the working parties did not really want to be there. They were either waiting to go on trade training courses, or they had just finished one and were awaiting another one or were waiting for release. There were various reasons, but they certainly did not want to be out in all weathers on working parties. This is where the word 'motivation' came in. You had to motivate the trainees to want to work, even though they were tired or not very good at it. Quite often there would be one of the senior officers, or chief officers, spying on the parties to make sure that they were not sitting around doing nothing. One of the ways I used to motivate the trainees was by working alongside them showing them how to do it. Usually, I could do it far better than them and I used to shame them into getting on with it. If the officer could do it, they thought, "well, I had better do it". The number of breaks they got depended on how hard they worked. One of the working parties, on a Monday, was scrubbing the floor of the Visitors' Hall. They used to have visits at weekends from their parents and friends and the hall had to be scrubbed out from top to bottom ready for the next weekend. Sometimes it would take two or three days depending on the size of the work party, but most of the trainees did not like scrubbing floors. I required them to scrub the traditional way, with a scrubbing brush and carbolic soap. Again, there would be

Dover Borstal

different officers in charge of this working party, and some had obviously let them swash dirty water over the floor to make it look as if it had been cleaned. This was not to my standard. I used to get down on my hands and knees and show them how to scrub a floor properly and say, "I do not care if you do not finish all the hall, but I want what you do finished, done properly." These were young lads, mainly 15-17 years olds, and they had never been led or controlled in this manner. I always found I could build a very good relationship with them if I was honest with them. I told them, "If we get the work done, or we work hard, we get breaks". If they did work hard, we would hide up and have a cigarette.

Often, when I was walking round the establishment, I would be looking out for work that needed doing. The parties were not that organised; they were just called Labour Party One, Labour Party Two and so on. It was up to the officer to find work, so I always had this in the back of my mind when walking around; there is a pile of bricks there, there is a load of dirt there, there is an area that needs sweeping. I also used to go round the training areas and ask the instructors if they had got work they wanted doing. Maybe the bricklayer wanted the yard cleaning up, or the welder had a heavy load of scrap metal he wanted clearing up. I would have all these in mind and so, when I got working parties, I always found I had work to do.

At Dover we worked variable shifts which could start at

6.00am in the morning and end up at 9pm. There were early shifts, late shifts, main shifts, and extended shifts. There was even one duty called Sleep Gate, where you literally slept on the gate, You used to get paid £2 if you came on at 9.00pm and went off at 6.00am. Technically you slept at the gate but quite often the gate was required to be opened for various emergencies or problems. If they needed keys, you quite often did not get a night's sleep. On occasions you would finish a long day shift, get put on the gate because no one had turned up for the shift, and then finish at half past six in the morning for an hour's break before coming back for another long day shift. Every six or seven weeks you did a week of nights where you patrolled the establishment, checked on the night patrols and the security of establishment, and were present for any problems either medical or other problems which may occur during the night. Usually, by midnight, the trainees had put their heads down and it was very quiet.

Family and friends often ask me if I was frightened working with large numbers of inmates, especially on my own. A lot of people think trainees behave as they did outside while they were inside, but criminals are not like that. Most trainees wanted to get through their sentence the best way they can. They do not behave irrationally all the time, although occasionally they would get involved in fights or arguments with members of staff. There were a few occasions when I was involved in disruptions. One was when I was in charge of the Church Party. There was a group of 50 trainees in the church hall and another 25 at a Roman Catholic service in the church. I had been advised by some trainees that there was going to be a punch up when the two parties got together for tea and coffee. I had advised the duty officer of what might take place and advised him to cancel the church evening, but he declined and told me to get on with it.

With only three staff what were we meant to do? As predicted, when the two parties joined together, a lot of arguing and shouting took place and very quickly things got out of hand. Chairs were thrown about, some going through the windows. I had observed the ringleader, so I rung the alarm, bear hugged this trainee and took him out of the room. On the way out I was hit over the back with a chair. Within a very short time more staff arrived, and the situation was brought under control. Another incident was when a large group of trainees were watching their monthly film in the visiting hall. Again, there were only three staff for over 100 trainees. When the lights were turned down chairs started to be thrown about. Fortunately, no one was hurt, and the situation was brought under control.

I also often get asked whether I got many injuries dealing with unruly inmates. My answer was, not often, because most trainees did not want to harm the staff. Usually, staff only got injured because they had got in the way. Another question I get asked quite often is, "How many times did you get assaulted?". I think people outside imagine that working in a prison is like working in a war zone, but most days, as far as that sort of things goes, it just does not happen.

Dover Borstal

Inmates, from time to time, will fight each other. Officers will try and break their fights up and sometimes get injured, but there were very few direct attacks on officers. Borstal boys would often deliberately fight in front of officers so that neither side would lose their pride when the fight was stopped by staff.

There was an incident where I had got my cheek bone broken tackling an escaped trainee who I spotted in Dover town centre. I had just drop Wendy off at the hairdressers and was walking up the High Street when I saw a trainee walking towards me, who I knew should have been at the hospital. I casually asked him what he was doing, thinking he would give himself up, but he looked round and punched me in the face. My head bounced off the lamp post behind me. As I fell, I grabbed him and wrestled him to the ground but, after a short time, he broke away, and ran down the High Street. Knowing the police station was just round the corner I went there and reported it to them. They told me they were aware that the trainee was missing and were looking into it, telling me to go to the hospital. When finally recaptured he received a further six months imprisonment.

Generally, the trainees complied with the rules and, if led correctly by the staff, they were only too pleased to obey the rules so that they get a better life. I often said to trainees, "If it was not for you, I would be out of a job so I'm glad you're here. If you make my life easy, I'll make your life easy". So, we had this sort of easy relationship most of the time. There were lines that they were not allowed to cross and some of these were a bit grey so you could be a bit flexible if you knew the inmate. One of the best ways to control trainees was to know their temperament and know a bit about them so you could deal with them.

Keeping control of a landing of thirty or forty trainees is not the best of jobs. You must keep on the go, keep alert, and keep one step ahead of them. When I was on the landing the trainees never knew when or where I was going to turn up. If they wanted to get up to any skulduggery, they had to be sure where I was. Being on the move enabled me to see what was going on and get a feel of the atmosphere and any tension. Reading the body language of the trainees was quite important. You could tell from a distance what sort of frame of mind he was in, so you could prepare yourself to deal with him as and when he came to you. Knowing the trainees was quite important as was them knowing you, so they knew which officers to approach for an honest answer. Quite often, officers would say they would do something, or tell them to come back later, or say that they could not have something. Trainees would try it on with other officers and see what reply they got. Quite often my first answer to a question from a trainee would be, "Have you asked any other member of staff?", and if they said, "Yes", I would say, "Well what did he say?". They would often respond, "No", and I said, "Well what do you think my answers going to be?". One of the annoying things about shift patterns is that sometimes you would go off duty at night, but you would not come back to the same unit the next morning. However, some officers would say, "Yeah I'll see you in the morning and I'll sort that out", but they were not going to be there, and this would cause ill-feeling with the inmates.

During the early 80s we had several pays rises and overtime payments were cancelled. From then on management had to ask you to work overtime with the promise of time off later. Pay increases were spread over a period and the salary was paid monthly into our bank account, rather than being paid weekly in cash. Over the year our pay was increased to a level where we did not miss the overtime. Hooray for family life! I was seeing my children on a regular basis. With the money we saved, we decided to move out of the quarters and buy our own house in Dover. We bought a modern house in a cul-de-sac which had belonged to the RSPCA. The owner had moved out a year previously and just used it for an office and for storing lost animals, so you can imagine what it looked like inside. We could see beyond the animal faeces and, as it was not selling, we got quite a large reduction in the price. We were able to have the house for a fortnight before moving in, to decorate it from top to bottom and have the coal fire taken out and a gas boiler put in. There is something about owning your own house. You can do things when you want without applying for permission. It was close enough to the shops and schools for our children to be able to walk if necessary and, with my reduction in hours, I was able to spend a lot more time with the family. Although the last three or four years had been hard work,

Dover Borstal

I was now starting to reap the rewards of all that I had put into it.

Strange as it may seem, I was really enjoying the job to the extent that I wanted to have more challenges. The day-to-day routine was an okay, but I wanted to get more out of the service through promotion, leadership roles and generally passing on my experiences to trainees and staff. It was now early 1982 and coming up for nearly four years' service, the time at which I could take the promotion exam, which I did and passed. I now had to wait for a promotion board, which I could apply for after seven years' service.

In early 1983 the Home Secretary was due to visit the establishment. This meant a general all-round tidy up. The Chief Officer wanted the marching of trainees to be improved, so he arranged a wing drill competition. I was selected to train Hythe House trainees. At first, I thought it would be a problem and nobody would want to take part. How wrong I was! Apart from a few dropping out I was left with 27, the smallest squad I could enter. They loved it and could not wait for me to come in on my own time to train them. After three weeks and a lot of fun the competition took place on the parade square, judged by an RSM from the local Guard's regiment. We won the drill competition and the Hythe House trainees got so excited that they carried me back to the wing on their shoulders. Unknown to them, there was a prize of £25, which I spent on fish and chips brought up from the town in newspaper for a supper.

Dover Borstal

At the supper I presented the best turned out trainees with half an ounce of tobacco, gold in those days.

This was what Borstal should be all about, getting trainees to work together and take responsibility for their behaviour. As I was a good hockey player, I arranged with the gym staff to let me take lads out on the weekends sport afternoon and show them that hockey was not only a girl game. After some basic stick training we played some team games. They loved it and wanted to play every weekend but due to staff shortages I could not arrange to be there every week and as the gym staff were not interested in hockey, it was dropped.

In my early days at Dover I always made Christmas a special day for the trainees. A lot of the trainees had not had a traditional Christmas with all the trimmings. So, a few days before, I would bring in decorations and a tree and get the trainees to help me set them up in the dining hall. The first time for a lot of them. Relatives and friends were allowed to send in small parcels, which were security checked, repacked in Christmas paper, and put under the Christmas tree. For the trainees with no parcels, house staff provided small presents for them. On Christmas Day we would let them stay in bed if they did not want to get up for breakfast. Most got up because it was the best breakfast of the year. During the morning, if the wing was cleaned to standard, they could come down for association until lunch, which was served by the staff. I often wore a dinner jacket and bow tie to serve them their meals. After lunch the chaplain would hand out the parcels from under the Christmas tree. In the afternoon, bingo was set up with small prizes such as soap, matches, cigarettes and sweets. This is what borstal was all about, building trust and relationships, gaining respect with the young trainees, and giving support from an adult which they may never have had before.

In 1983, Dover was still a borstal, but changes were coming. Up until then, trainees had to earn their release date, serving an indeterminate sentence of 6 months to 2 years. Each month trainees would have a house report done. Anyone who had come into contact with the trainee could submit a report for consideration, good or bad. Sometimes family and friends of trainees would write in and say how much he had changed. At the monthly meetings a decision would be made to give the trainee a week back, stay on target, or lose a week. All trainees would start their sentence with a target date of nine months. This meant a lot to most trainees, so, at the end of each month, many trainees would become extra helpful, thinking we would forget their previous behaviour. The system worked, trainees who worked hard and showed respect got discharged early, others stayed longer.

However, in mid-1983 the borstal system was abolished and replaced with Young Offenders Institutes, or YOIs for short. A sad day. It was said that borstal did not work. I disagreed. Most of the lads left with improved education, trade skills and better respect for authority. Where it fell down was the support after release. The big change was the sentence arrangement. It was brought into line with adult sentencing, i.e., fixed term with fixed remission. The difference being inmates did not have to earn release, they just had to stay out of trouble. Another big difference was that all prison officers wore uniform. So, we all went off duty one day and the next we returned in full uniform. However, it made little difference to our relationship with inmates. It is the person in the uniform not the uniform that gets respect.

Due to overcrowding, Hythe House reverted to a training wing. New receptions went straight to their allocated wings from reception. The other big difference was they were called 'inmates' now, but to me, as they will always be trainees. They could return time after time until they were 21, unless their sentence was over five years. This may not seem a problem, but returning inmates were familiar with the systems and played on their past experience; because they were not all first timers the job got more challenging but also more interesting. The Personal Officer scheme was introduced at about the same time. This required officers to be allocated to several inmates, and they became the first point of contact when on duty. Officers had to build up a closer relationship with their allocated inmates and liaise with other departments on their behalf both inside and out.

In early 1984 my duties were moved to the gate and operations officer. This meant losing regular contact with

Dover Borstal

inmates, but I had no choice. As the gate officer I was responsible for the security of all keys in the establishment and the recording of all personnel and vehicles coming in and out, an easy, but, at times, boring job. When not working at the gate I would be working as communications officer in the Duty Officer's room, a more interesting job. It required me to control the prison radio network, issue and withdraw radios, and man the telephone switchboard. This could be very demanding when there was an incident going on around the establishment. After nearly two years working on the gate and communications I returned to Hythe House, back working with inmates. I had tried to work my overtime hours on the house blocks maintaining my contact with inmates. I was selected to go on a Personal Officer training course, so that on return I could train discipline staff. The course was very interesting and enabled me to put my interpretation on my life experiences to a better use. Getting to know the individual inmate was very important. Not an easy task, when the inmates ranged from immature 15-year-olds, to a know it all 21-year-olds. Staff needed time to get to know their allocated inmates, a problem I fought hard to resolve.

With the changes going on, the education staff stopped pre-release training; the course they had to attend two weeks before release, whether they needed it or not. Again, I was selected to go on a pre-release training course with a view to taking over and training discipline staff for this course.

Dover Borstal

Although I was still a basic officer, I was spending more and more time acting up to senior officer and arranging training programmes for staff and inmates. On one occasion I was asked to run a course for the Prince's Youth Trust. The idea was that, as most inmates found it difficult to get employment on release. With this course they could be trained to run their own businesses; so technically employing themselves. With the aid of some specialists in business management, I ran a six-week course for 13 inmates. Most of the inmates found it very interesting and knuckled down to the hard work put in front of them. On later release one inmate set up a business videoing weddings, another doing pallet reclaiming and a third making and selling sandwiches around factories. Unfortunately, this was only a trial and nothing else came out of it.

These experiences were to hold me in good stead on my promotion board in 1987. When I got the result, I had passed. I was now required to select a posting to a new establishment. After talking it through with Wendy we decided that we were happy to move away from Dover and I applied for three different establishments around the country. Would you believe, I was promoted in-situ at Dover? I was moved from Hythe House to Romney House into the role of senior officer.

Being a senior officer in those days was a challenge, not only with inmates, but also with the management of basic grade staff. As a senior officer you wore a white shirt and a pip on each shoulder whilst the basic grade officers wore blue shirts. The role of senior officer was to supervise the other staff on the wing, ensuring inmates kept themselves, their rooms and the communal areas clean and tidy. You had to maintain security checks, keep accurate rolls of inmate movements, communicate with the main control centre and other areas of the prison, whilst also solving inmate's problems and behaviour as and when required. Some of the young officers also needed support to deal with the more mature inmates. There was never a dull moment and no time to get bored.

By the late 1980s I was spending more and more time running training courses, pre-release for inmates and Personal Officer Scheme training for staff. I was able to change the pre-release training, altering it from being delivered not only near the end of their sentence but when and if it was appropriate earlier in their sentence. This was achieved by restricting it to only those inmates who needed the training. I found a good 80% of inmates lacked communication skills. With the aid of a video camera, I was able to show them what they looked like when communicating. With the aid of various games, using questions and answers, many of them improved their skills. A course called, 'Fend for Yourself', always went down well. This helped them to be more useful when returning home to family and friends. The training involved learning simple tasks such as changing a fuse, fitting a new electrical plug, bleeding a radiator and cooking a cheap nutritious meal on a small Belling cooker. There were all useful things when living on your own. Sometimes, I was requested to go to other establishments to help them carry out this type of training.

As part of my duties, I was also required to cover for the absence of the Training and the Security Principal Officer. This required me to arrange and deliver training sessions to all grades of staff. I also had to give talks to new local magistrates. Their view was often that prison does not work as over 60% reoffend. I agreed with them, if they only measured success by reoffending, but I explained that I did not measure it this way. Most inmates go out more able to cope with the outside environment, with improved education, trade skills, fitness and more respect for authority. The reason they failed was they get little support on the outside after release; this was not a failing of the prison service.

While covering for the Principal Officer, or 'acting up' as it was called, I was required to be in charge of the establishment after the governor grades went off duty. This meant dealing with all the incidents as well as a finalising role and key checks before handing over to the night staff. It also meant opening the establishment in the morning and ensuring there was adequate staff to man the prison for the day as shortages of staff meant less time out the cells for inmates. I was enjoying these new responsibilities, the best of both worlds I would say. Contact with inmates, training, and using my leadership skills.

Dover Borstal

My family life was about to change again. In 1989 we sold our house in Dover and moved back to Folkestone. I still worked in Dover and Wendy was also based there and the move meant we both had to travel daily. This was mostly okay but was not so good in bad weather. However, we felt that it was worthwhile because of ongoing problems we were having with the neighbours. Once again, I had promotion in my sights. I would be applying for a board shortly and I thought the extra management responsibilities I had taken on would help my chances.

In 1990 there was a lot of new prisons being built and they needed more trained staff. The Prison Service were setting up an extra training course at Hull University during the university summer recess and needed extra tutors to run the courses. I applied and had to go to the Staff College and present a 20-minute talk on any subject. I chose the Personal Officer Scheme. It appeared to go down well, and I got one of the 25 places. This meant going up to the service college in Rugby for two weeks training and then on to Hull to teach the 10 week course. The training ranged from marching, communication skills, all aspects of security, report writing, and all the other skills a prison officer would need. Fortunately, it was a Monday to Friday job, and I could travel home at weekends. I thoroughly enjoyed my time there, especially the interaction with the new staff. During one session I had someone from head office sit in and after they said, "You made a dreary subject sound interesting". Two of the officers on my section were posted to Dover so they would have to put up with me for a bit longer.

Shortly after my return from Hull University, I was called up for a promotion board, which I passed. All I could think of now was where I was going to be posted. This time it would be away from Dover, with my wife working locally and my son approaching the start of his studies for his GCSE's, it made sense for us to stay in our current house and for me to do the travelling. To make this possible I applied for a posting to any Kent prison.

After 14 years at Dover I was, in some ways, sad to leave. It was both the end of an era and a new challenge as I would inevitably be working with adult prisoners. Had all my efforts been worthwhile? Yes! Just to see young lads become men, better equipped to survive in the outside world. Looking back over those years I have many fond memories. Such as, meeting an ex-inmate in Dover Town Centre and being introduced to his wife and family. He said to his wife, "This is Mr. Culpin who taught me to go straight many years ago. I have got a family, a job, and a council house and a lot of it is down to you". I replied, "Well done, keep it up", and went on my way with a broad smile on my face. I will always remember the time I had to deal with a young lad who was threatening to hang himself. He was standing on the heating pipes with a noose around his neck attached to the window bars. After talking to him for some time he got upset, slipped on the pipes and was hanging by the noose. I quickly got to him, took the weight of his body and cut the noose from around his neck. Another memory was the time a young inmate came to me crying and said he was being bullied all the time and asking me to help him. I explained to him the way I had dealt being with bullied at his age; I would tell them if they carried on, I would get them when they were not looking. The inmate said thank you and went back to work. A short while later I was told that this young inmate had hit another inmate over the head with a shovel. I was concerned I would be in trouble for what I had said to him, but on speaking to him later, he confirmed that had said nothing to anyone about our conversation. From that day onwards he was never bullied again!

HMP Elmley

It was now 1992 and my new posting was HMP Elmley on the Isle of Sheppey, 52 miles from Folkestone. Elmley was newly built, just completed and awaiting new staff and inmates. It was an adult male prison taking inmates from the local magistrates and crown courts. I was to take on the role of Operations Manager, a complex job with many areas of responsibility. To start with I received new staff arriving weekly, mostly from the national training school, to whom I had to give an induction period and allocate to the new wings as they opened. Newly trained staff made up 80% of the overall staff. A challenge on its own! Elmley prison was very much larger than anything I had experienced before. It would hold over 600 inmates when full, with over 250 staff. Apart from the four large inmate cell blocks there was a large hospital, laundry, education centre, visitors' complex, gym, multi-use workshops, reception centre and a large administration complex. Elmley was to be used as a local prison, this meant taking in a large range of prisoners, from life sentence prisoners, down to remand prisoners. There was also a special wing for sex offenders. In other words, a complete and complex mix.

For the first few months a lot of my work was done by

HMP Emley

trial and error. Building routines and training staff to meet the needs of the new prison. I also had to attend many management meetings with the Governor and his Senior Management Team. As the inmates started to arrive, I took over the responsibilities for inmate visiting arrangements, including legal visits, reception centre and the segregation block. One other duty I had to take on was Duty Officer. Most of the work for this was after normal working hours, when the senior staff had gone home, and you were left to deal with any emergencies.

There were three deaths during my time at Elmley, a suicide in a hospital, and two from heart attacks during the evening. A 'Care Team', made up of the Chaplain and nursing staff, had been set up to support staff and inmates when this sort of incident happened. As Duty Officer I had to call in the care team on these three occasions. The problem I saw was that none of the team had close experience of working with inmates. When there was an incident, I always ensured that staff and inmates got full support, ensuring they were fit to carry on their duties. Often the Care Team would persuade some of the staff to go off duty with stress, totally undermining the work I had already done. It was often the case when new procedures were put in place there was a lack of thought into how they work in practice, making a manager's job that more difficult.

There was only one escape during my stay at Elmley, it could well have been part of the script of a TV programme like *Porridge*. Two inmates stowed away in a laundry van evading both the staff in the laundry, the driver and gate staff. If the staff had carried out the correct procedure it would not have happened, a learning curve for those staff. If the driver had stayed with his van whilst it was loaded and not been persuaded by the inmates to go for a cup of tea, it would not have happened. The gate keeper relied on the driver having done his job because the van was full to the roof with bags of laundry and not easy to search. This had been a pre-arranged escape. Both men cut their way out of the van and were met by a car and got off the island before the road bridge closed. One of them was caught after a few days; the other one got to France and had the cheek to request his property be sent on!

In 1993 a new staffing arrangement was introduced, in line with new government policies, whereby 25 per cent of all staff, in male prisons had to be female. We were told of this arrangement without any input from existing staff. Several procedures would have to change, especially when it involved common decency and privacy for inmates: for example, when using the toilets, washing, or strip searching. Not an easy task when there was a shortage of staff, or when a number of male staff were on annual leave or sick. There were also more practical problems. For example, when they built new prisons, they only considered the needs of inmates. There were no rest areas for staff inside or out. There were no staff toilets on the wings and male officer used the inmates' toilets. When female officers were introduced, this became a problem because they had to be off the wings to go to the toilet. The first intake of new female staff are either newly promoted or looking for promotion. Apparently due to the small number of female prisons it was difficult to get promotion, hence a move to male establishments. I was not against this new procedure as I felt that female staff were, on average, as good if not better than male staff in some situations. Female officers were often able to calm the male inmates down as they did not want to feel stupid in front of them where a male officer might have inflamed the situation. In 1994 a female deputy governor was appointed. She appeared from the outset to favour female staff, to the extent of calling female only staff meetings. When asked why this was, she said that females could not talk about male officers in front of them. My reply to this was to request male only meetings. A difficult position for the Governor, but he replied that, where possible, all staff should be encouraged to attend any meetings for their grade. However, this should not stop individual staff requesting a meeting with any manager. What I call a cop out!

In 1995 I was approached by the area manager with a request to go to HMP Aldington to sort out a serious security problem that they had. This prison was the only 9 miles from where I lived and would reduce my travelling by 86 miles a day. It was an offer I could not refuse. Elmley prison had given me a lot of confidence and experience at a management level but working in a large prison did not suit my style. I had often felt isolated from the main work of a prison, dealing with inmates. As I had reached my promotion potential, I was more interested in being involved in the day-to-day work of a prison. However, I would also have to get used to working at a more senior management level.

HMP Aldington

In 1995 I moved to HMP Aldington. I was now 54 years old and had gained a good all-round experience of prison life. Aldington was a small, category C prison that took inmates who were either near the end of their sentence, or only doing a short sentence with a low category security risk. The prison itself was an old prisoner of war camp for German prisoners who used it to sleep there after working on the nearby farms. It consisted of a row of wooden huts convert it into dormitories. It was completely unsuitable as a modern prison. No wonder they had a security problem; even the outer fence was more like a garden fence than a prison fence! The prison held up to 147 inmates and was staffed by 27 basic grade officers, four senior officers, one principal officer, and two governor grades. The prison was also supported by several civilian staff.

Overall, the inmates where well behaved, keen to keep busy and complete their sentences. There was a large education centre, a manufacturing workshop, extensive grounds, and a lot of requests for inmates to work out in the community. The outgoing principal officer was still there when I first arrived. He appeared to be less than useless. He was a national union representative and had spent most of his working hours away from the prison. No wonder the prison was falling apart!

I spent the first few weeks talking to staff and finding out what kept the place ticking over. It was clear that the Governor had little idea how to manage a prison and, if it had not been for a few dedicated staff, the whole place would have fallen apart. In the last few years there had been two security audits in which the prison had failed to meet the standards required. After several meetings with the Governor, it became clear to me he was not interested and was expecting a move and downgrade shortly. So, he told me to get on with it. There was a Deputy Governor, who I knew from working with him at Dover. He was very laid back and only a few months from retirement, so he was also happy to let me get on with it.

The prison was due to be expanded, taking in a lot of the farm fields surrounding the existing fence and replacing this with a high security fence. There was talk that Aldington was likely to become an Immigration Centre in the near future; but this was only rumour. This would most likely be years ahead and I had to work based on what it was like now. Within my first year there the new fence was completed; this work included a proper secure gate with entrances for vehicles and pedestrians. A new visitors' centre was also built with a separate entrance for visitors. The old centre had been the cause of a lot of contraband being smuggled in. I had a separate locker room built to hold visitors' property and they could only take in a small amount of cash to buy tea and biscuits. I also had CCTV fitted in the main visiting hall, with a member of staff monitoring the cameras during visits.

The Security Department was run by spare staff, who searched inmates, their sleeping areas, and all other areas of the prison either at random or on security information. I encourage all staff, to report any unusual behaviour, however small, to the security department. A few small issues could lead to a big security problem. The CCTV in the visiting hall had cut down most of the smuggling in of drugs and other unauthorized items. On top of these precautions, I arranged a drugs dog to do random searching of all visitors before entering the prison. This resulted in several police prosecutions. In 1996 Mandatory Drug Testing, or MDT as it was called, was brought in. This required all the inmates to submit to regular drug testing. To do this I had a secure room built in place of my old office. The team, including myself, had the necessary training to legally carry out these tests. Tests were carried out randomly or on security information. The tests required inmates to supply a urine sample which then tested for drugs and if found positive sent away to laboratory for confirmation. If confirmed the inmate would be placed on Governor's Report and usually returned to a more secure prison.

Up to my arrival, the four senior officers had no designated job description and just took charge of the inmates' accommodation block. As this only required one senior officer at a time, there was a lot of spare hours I could put to good use. I organised one senior officer to take responsibility for security and the detailing of staff duties, and the other for training and outside activities, both reporting to me regularly. Up to 20 inmates were temporarily released each day to work out in the community. This meant doing stringent security checks, not only on the inmates, but also checking on the work locations to see if the employer had any security issues. If any of the inmates did not return, I was answerable to the Governor. During the three years I was there, only three failed to return, all of them had problems at home which I could not have known about in advance.

In mid-1996 a new governor was posted in. He had been my deputy governor at Dover. Like me, he liked to get involved at all levels, but mostly left me to my own devices if I kept him up to date with what was going on at any one time. In late 1996, Aldington received yet another security audit, but this time receiving a good grade which boosted the morale of all the staff. We had now become a real prison. However, there was still work to be done. I introduced interviews for all new arriving inmates. This was to ensure that they had no major problems. It was an opportunity to introduce them to Aldington and what it could do for them; encouraging them to make the best of their time here. Most inmates did just that, but there were a few who had been moved sideways because they had been troublemakers in their old establishments. These had to be monitored very carefully because we did not have facilities, such as secure cells to put them in.

I was kept very busy, working alterative weekends and covering the duties of Governor when either one was off sick or on leave, which happen quite often. I also had to carry out night visits and be on call for incidents such as attempted escapes, inmate disruption and staffing problems. Fortunately, I was not called out often. Most of the inmates just completed their sentences and were released. However, there were one or two inmates who had been transferred because of problems they had in their previous establishment. One of which I remember because he was a lottery winner of £1.4 million pounds. I gave him stern warning about his behaviour, such as paying other inmates to smuggle a mobile phone and drugs into the prison. The local and national media were aware of this inmate and kept hassling the gate keeper for information of his whereabouts. After a short time, it was clear he was not suitable for this type of prison and so I arranged a transfer. I told him he would be transferred the next day, knowing he would get the information to the press. Instead, I transferred him that night. In the morning there was a lot of disappointed cameramen and press reporters when I told them he had already gone.

In the prison there was an industrial workshop, employing up to 25 inmates. Large, part moulded rubber sheets were delivered to the prison by British Rail. They had to be cut into blocks to make rail insulators. This was hard work for which inmates got extra pay. At one time the instructor in the shop became difficult and would not operate the forklift to load and unload supplies. I took it in hand by obtaining the necessary qualification myself to operate the lift. Problem solved!

By 1997 the Governor was having longer periods of sick leave requiring me to take on more and more of the Governor's responsibilities. I attended several areas and national governors' meetings, sometimes in London. The area manager turned up one day when the Governor was away and started questioning me about him such as what I thought of him, was he doing a good job etc? I told him I would only talk about him in his presence. He commended me for my loyalty.

Also, in 1997, another security audit was announced. By this time, I felt that Aldington had nothing to fear. We were ready for anything they could throw at us. We received notification that we had one of the best security standards on the country. As a result, I was requested to go to a small prison in Hampshire to show them how it should be done, a very pleasing time for me. On return I spent a lot of time writing the policy statement on security procedures for Aldington, getting the Governors approval and publishing them in the staff room at the gate for all staff to read. This was how it would be done at Allington; my interpretation of how staff would carry out Prison Security Regulations.

The last two years had certainly been challenging but I had enjoyed it, mostly because I could put many of my ideas into practice. It was now time to put my training skills to good use. I set up promotion class for those eligible and security update training for all staff including civilians. Some of the training was in my own time but was appreciated by the staff who had mostly forgotten what training was about. Most prison did not give civilian staff regular security training, but I felt it was important. Around this time a new wing for inmates was built and with some negotiating I had it made into single rooms for inmates who worked outside daily. They had their own room keys, which could be double locked by staff, making it a good steppingstone to release. It was also used for early workers in the kitchen. This stopped them disturbing the other inmates.

I had a good family life, with my daughter married and living in Milton Keynes, and my son was doing well at the local grammar school preparing himself for his A levels. Wendy and I were able to take regular holidays, mostly abroad. In early 1998 I was asked to go on a governor grade promotion board. I felt I had reached the grade level I was comfortable with, and I had no more aspirations for promotion. However, I attended the board because I had nothing to lose. Surprise, surprise I did not pass! This, I felt, was due to my outspoken attitude; not what they wanted at Governor grade. They were just looking for a yes man.

At about this time I read an advertisement on the Home

Office notices that retired principal officers were sought to join the Cayman Island Prison Service[5]. As I was not retired, I did not think it applied to me. However, when I got home, I mentioned it to Wendy who quickly replied, "Are you putting in for it then?". I had no idea she would be interested but on hearing this response I decided to investigate it further and I found it could apply to me. Staff over 55 and with over 20 years' service could retire on full pension and gratuities. Wendy was also able to retire on full pension, enabling us to pay off our mortgage and rent or close up our home and spend two or more years in the sun. As I only had under 3 years to compulsory retirement at 60, it was a serious consideration. Wendy was going through a very stressful time at work and could not wait to leave, but first, I had to be selected for the post.

On submitting an application, I was called to the Cayman Island office in London for an interview. This turned out to be very intensive with a panel made up of the Cayman Prison Director (Governor) and a government minister from the island. They quizzed me on all aspects of my experience. Not being afraid to speak out, I felt I gave a good account of myself. Unknown to me at the time there were 300 applicants for the two posts. What chance did I have!? Within two weeks I had a phone call to say that I had been accepted for one of the posts to start in June/July 1998. I now needed to do a lot of research, could I retire

---

[5] British Crown Colony in the West Indies.

in time, could I afford to live on the Cayman Islands, and would my wages cover the cost of living? It was clearly an expensive place to live, although there was no income tax and the government workers got free Medical Health cover.

After extensive research I was convinced, we could make a go of it. Our pensions would cover the cost of leaving our house in Folkestone locked up and not rented. This left a base to come home to if things did not turn out as we expected or a place to stay on breaks back in the UK. Our son was at university and so could come out during his holidays if he wanted. We decided to give it a go. The only problem was Wendy could not retire until October and I had to take up the post in July, meaning three months of separation. After some sleepless nights we still thought it was a chance of a lifetime that we would never have again. One advantage was I would have plenty of time to set up a home for Wendy to come out to. So, after a thorough medical, I signed up for a two-year contract and retired from the British Prison Service with effect from the end of June 1998. In some ways I was sorry to leave. Over the last three years I had put a lot of hard work into helping to bring Aldington up to a high standard. Unknown to me, the prison was to close two years later due to government cutbacks. I felt a lot of hard work was wasted. If I had known, would I have worked so hard? Yes, of course, I always work hard!

⛓ HMP Northward ⛓

After a short holiday in Tenerife, I booked a single flight leaving for the Cayman Islands on 1st of July 1998. With some regret, I left Wendy to close the house and join me in the following October. All the family came to Gatwick to see me off. I had little idea what to expect when I arrived, other than that the Cayman Island Government would pay for four nights' accommodation in an hotel and then I would be on my own. Even with my experience overseas, this was going to test me. I had been able to contact the other new officer, called Frank, and found out he had arrived with his wife in June. He agreed to meet me at the airport and pass on the knowledge he had already gained.

With two huge travel bags, and after a 12-hour flight, I arrived in George Town, the capital of Grand Cayman. It was late evening and hot and humid. As agreed, Frank was there to meet me and take me to the hotel. He was still living in an hotel but due to move out into a rented house shortly. After a restless night I was taken to the prison, HMP Northward, which was to be my workplace for the next two years. I met the Director and senior staff, was measured for my uniform, which was made in the prison, and was told to come back in four days.

It would be hard enough in the UK to rent a house, sign up for utilities, buy a car, and get it licensed in four days. Was it possible in the Cayman Islands? Some islanders said no, because the whole pace of life here is very slow. It was a good job I was up for a challenge. I first rented a car and, on reading an advertisement in the local paper, I found an ideal house within my price range and arrange a viewing later that day. The property was on a complex called Palm Springs It had two bedrooms, 2 1/2 bathrooms and air conditioning. There was a communal swimming pool, tennis courts and a large area for parking. It was only 200 yards from a white sandy beach. What more could I ask for? The owners were from the UK but had lived on the island for years. They were keen to rent to a reliable tenant on a long lease. I was able to sign up for two years at an agreed price, not cheap, but I could afford it. Best of all, it was fully furnished and, if I could get the utilities signed up, I could move in on Friday, four days after arrival. For the next two days I chased about, queuing for hours, pleading with the counter staff to get the electricity, water and telephone put on by Friday. With a lot of charm and wit I did it. I even had time to buy and licence a second-hand car and hand the rented car back. Didn't I do well! Unknown to me, Frank had moved into the same complex the day before. It had taken him over three weeks!

I updated Wendy several times during these first few days by phone, which I found out to be very expensive and hoped in future to use the prison phone system. Shortly after moving in, I took lots of pictures of the house and surrounding area and sent them to Wendy to show her what she was coming out to. During the first weekend I was able to explore the island. What a wonderful place. White sandy beaches, sea full of fish, and coconut trees everywhere. I hoped that when Wendy came out, she would love it. The local food was strange and very spicy, but European Food was available at a price in George Town. Most products sold on the island were imported, incurring an import tax of 20 per cent. In other words, they were expensive!

Now my thoughts turned to work and what was expected of me. The prison staff was made up of two directors, four principal officers, four lead officers and eighty officers. So far, I only knew that I was joining the Management Team. On a further meeting with the Director, I was told I was to take up the post of Programmes Manager. On asking him for a job description he said he had no idea what the job entailed but was told he needed one and that was why I was here. I requested some time to investigate the needs of the prison and write a job description accordingly. He agreed.

It was clear that prison procedures were very out of date compared with the UK. They had not advanced since the prison was opened in the 1980's. Northward was the only prison on the island and was located about 10 miles from the capital, George Town. It took remands and sentenced prisoners, both male and female, and a few who were sent to prison because they were found insane. Sentences ranged from a few weeks to life, which, unlike the UK, actually meant for the rest of their lives. There were about 30 female and 200 male prisoners. The staff consisted of about 100 male and female officers with a collection of civilians. The accommodation wings were made of solid concrete, with some two-man cells and several large dormitories, the largest of which housed nearly 60 inmates. All sleeping areas had internal sanitation with several open toilets and showers. The boundary of the prison had a high double fence with a castle-like gate entrance. The Director had his own house and an office outside the fence.

Where was I going to start? Frank took the role of Security Manager, again, no job description. I decided to start with getting to know and understand the culture of the inmates and staff, as it was so very different from that in the UK. I quickly circulated myself around the different departments talking to everyone I met and letting them know I was here to help. I said to them all, "if you have problems let me know and I will try and solve them". I am not sure they understood why I was here, but they let me get on with it.

There were several working areas where inmates could keep themselves busy during their sentence. These consisted of a large vegetable garden, carpentry workshop, pottery shop, tailor shop, laundry, education classrooms and large grounds to be kept clean and tidy. There was also a large maintenance workshop which employed several skilled inmates. All in all, there was a good nucleus of work for inmates, it just needed better organizing. Outside there was a farm for chickens, rabbits, and a good selection of fruit trees. Inmate visits were held between the two main gates.

This was the only safe place at the time. The gate was built like a small fort and was the only entrance to the prison, it housed reception, medical centre, management and admin offices. There was an inner and outer gate, of which only one could be open at a time. Visitors used the small side gate as the large main gates were not allowed to be opened during visits. Not ideal, but it worked.

On visiting the various work areas, I found the woodworking shop was run by an officer and was turning out good quality furniture; but I was not sure where these products were going. I later found out he was making units for his friends' houses; something I would investigate. The pottery shop was run by whoever turned up, mostly a lifer [6]and was underutilised. They made some amazing pieces, including mugs, cups and ornaments etc. The shelves around the shop were full to overflowing due to there being no organized outlet to recover the costs. This would have to change. The education centre was run by a civilian teacher who was not very happy with me prowling around his domain. The laundry was run by a civilian who appeared to be doing a good job, supported by four lifer inmates.

The grounds parties, of which there were three, were a bit of a hit and miss. There was nobody with overall responsibility for what was going on. However, due to the skill and keenness of several of the inmates, there was some large vegetable beds which were full of great looking crops,

---

6 An inmate serving a whole life sentence

enough to supply the kitchen and more. The outside farm was run by an officer and civilian who employed up to 10 security vetted inmates. The farm consisted of long two-tiered chicken cages holding up 2500 chickens and 100 rabbits, surrounded by many unkempt fruit trees. It was clear that the prison had the potential to make money if an outlet could be found for their products; something I was going to investigate.

The female wing was fenced off from the main prison and run by female officers. There were large, beautiful grounds with well-kept flowerbeds and fruit trees. In fact, it looked like a holiday camp, compared to the male section. The female wing had a small workshop which produced products such as handbags, slippers and an assortment of sewn and knitting items. Again, there was a full store cupboard and no outlet for sales.

The prison had a very laid-back attitude and surprisingly few problems of indiscipline. Were two white officers going to change this? I hoped not and would do my best to get them on my side by looking for areas of change that would benefit them, without unnecessary changes to their past methods. Inmates pay was a good starting point. They all seemed to get the same amount of money for however long they did or did not work. This made a lot of inmates uninterested in working, many were just happy to sit around the wings. After a meeting with the Director, I had convinced him I could come up with a better system and make a saving on his budget. I would use a point base system where work areas were graded according to their skill and number of hours worked. The person in charge of the party awarded points of between one and five for each morning or afternoon shift. It took a lot of time convincing the inmates they would benefit from hard work. "Points made prizes", I said. I worked out what the system would cost and presented it to the Director who, when realising it would save several $1000 a year and accepting that the inmates were happy with the system, reluctantly let me introduce it. After a few teething problems the system worked well and the inmates quickly learnt that those who worked, got paid! Up to now all working party were allocated on a first come first serve, this meant that the long-term prisoners stopped any new inmates getting experience and improving their skills. So, I arranged for at least one space on every party to be used as a six-week training session and then reallocated. Inmates could then apply for a full-time place.

My next challenge was to set up a display at the next government departments' get together. Apparently, this was done annually, although the prison had not been represented for some years. The aim was to get a better understanding of the workings of the individual departments, with the aim of improving relationships. In the short time I had been on the island it was apparent that the prison was a case of out of sight out of mind. Hopefully I would change this and build good relationships with other government departments. My aim was to display as many products as possible. The wood shop made miniature chicken and rabbit hutches with a view to taking orders for the full-size versions. On the Sunday of the event, with the help of two other staff, I set up two large wooden screens covered in photographs and notices on what the prison was all about in the main government building car park. Also, two large tables were laid out and covered in a large selection of items made by both male and female inmates. Because I could not have a real inmate present, I dressed up a dummy of an inmate with a notice saying, "What the well-dressed prisoner is wearing this year". The whole display drew a lot of attention, and we took a lot of orders for products. The Director stayed away but took the praise when the local paper recorded how good the prison display was. Very quickly we started getting orders from government departments for the prison products, some saying that until seeing our display, they had not known that the prison made these items. The prison began making money, something that was unheard of in the past. I arranged for a prison stall to be set up on all the island craft and food fairs. Arrangements were even made to use the steps of the High Court in the main town square once a year. This was ideal for attracting the multitude of American tourists who visited the island on cruise ships.

Whilst these initiatives were successful, it was time I had a meeting with the Director with a view to getting a better understanding of what I was trying to do. I assured him I was not after his job; my only aim was to serve him and use my experience to improve the general standards of the prison in areas where he wanted it done. I asked him to take advantage of me as I was only here for two years. He seemed pleased with what I had said and from then on our relationship improved.

The three months separation from my wife was coming to an end. After a last-minute scare, because Wendy was not well, she recovered in time to fly out during the first week of October 1998. I had missed her a lot and could not wait to see her again. During this time, I had been able to repaint the lower floor of the rented house and make it ready for her. On her arrival I took two days leave to show off the island to her, hoping she would like this island paradise.

Back at work I continued to make changes. Before I arrived, all inmates were drug tested each month, all 300 of them in two days. This was impossible if done correctly and cost several $1000 at a time. What a waste! Inmates knew when they were going to be tested so could prepare for it. I persuaded the Director to trial the system used in the UK, one of random testing and acting on security information. Within a few months the system was working well and saving the budget thousands of dollars and still getting the same results. In reality, not a lot of drugs were being used.

I introduced a reception interview for every new inmate. Up until now new inmates were allocated to a wing and left to their own devices. Most of the interviews were done by me and were appreciated by the inmates. I explained to them what was expected of them in terms of behaviour, what was available to improve their education and skills and how to sort out any problems. The staff and inmates were getting used to my methods and knew they were always welcome to speak to me. When on duty I would ensure I was present during the mealtimes to show that I was around. I would talk to inmates, something I felt was important. There was a fenced sports field that was hardly used, so at least once a week I took two football teams out, mainly young offenders, and refereed the game myself. This resolved a standing complaint that referees drawn from the inmates were biased. If I was on duty on Sunday mornings, I always attended the church service, inviting Wendy on one occasion. There was no proper church within the prison and the main dining hall was used. This changed when some the local church groups had raised money to build a church on top of the kitchen and dining hall. They provided the building materials, and the prison inmates provided the skills and labour. Fortunately, we had several builders serving time who got together and built a wonderful church. No way could this been built in a UK prison; but who needs health and safety? They just got the job done.

From time to time, I would have to adjudicate on inmates reported for offences against prison rules. This was run like a court, with witnesses called when required. If found guilty they could lose time, money, or be put in the cell block for several days. My previous training was put to good use; I had been trained in adjudication procedures and knew how to conduct a hearing in a legal and fair manner. This has not always been the case in the past and so at one stage inmates who had offended would ask me to be the person to adjudicate. If an inmate wanted to appeal against the sentence it was done to the Director. I only had one appeal against my sentence and that just happen to be the Director's son who was serving time for a drug offence. He was found with a mobile phone which had been smuggled in by the Director's ex-wife. Believe it or not the Director dismissed the case on appeal!

Wendy was having a problem settling down, mostly boredom, I think. On seeing an advertisement for new members required to join the island's International Ladies Club, I persuaded her to phone and join. With this, and the purchase of another car, she never looked back and before long was making new friends and going out all over the island. She made good friends with the Police Commissioner wife, whose husband was on secondment from the British police. For our first Christmas on the island my son came out and joined us during his university break. We booked a Christmas lunch in the best hotel, right on the beach. Frank and his family also joined us, and we had a great day; even a swim in the sea after. There may have been a cloud in the sky, but I never saw it. At around this time I took an open water sea diving course, because I did not want to waste these beautiful seas full of wonderful fish and coral. On my days off Wendy and I spent hours travelling round the island, sitting on the beaches and swimming in the pool in at the house.

In the New Year, with the Director's permission, I

set up monthly staff meetings. The purpose was to pass on important information and hear first-hand their daily problems. Overall, they went down well, even the Director attended on some occasions. The one problem I had was the old Caribbean culture of always turning up late. To overcome this, I advertise the meetings half an hour before required and gave out tea and biscuits. Problem solved!

Although there was a good training room outside the prison, training was non-existent. Most staff had received no further training for years; something I hope to change. Most of the management grades had computers but had not been trained to use them, so they got little use. I knew of two inmates who had worked in the banking industry and were very good with computers. So, with the Directors permission, I arranged computer classes for staff during the lunch period. At first the staff were not happy with inmates training them, but I persuaded the Director to attend the first session and he was quickly joined by the other staff. Overall, my hard work and persuasive personality was paying off.

The inmate population had increased to its highest. The numbers had gone up almost daily since I had been there, but the staff numbers and accommodation space remained the same. The prison was originally built to house up to 120 inmates. The roll now stood at close to 300. Dormitories made for 20 inmates now had 40 and more; single cells had two or three inmates. There was a Segregation Unit, or Punishment Block as it was sometimes called. It was built to take up to 10 inmates, but now had 46. This included 10 inmates in a room originally designed to carry out executions, by hanging[7]. The trap door for the drop was covered over and the room fitted out with 6 bunk beds. This level of overcrowding was bound to cause problems. I had to give up my office as it was in an unused cell, and a 40-foot container was brought into the prison and converted into two offices; one for me and the other for Frank. I requested it to be put in a fenced area just inside the main gates. However, for reasons unknown to me, it was set up at the far end of the prison compound. Not a very secure area, but we had to make the best of it.

In early April 1999 Wendy and I decided to take a holiday back in the UK for three weeks and return to the island with Wendy's parents who were in their eighties. Within four days of returning, I was to get the shock of my life.

---

[7] The island stopped capital punishment in the 1990s and commuted these sentences to life imprisonment.

Our New Home

Meeting one of the locals

It still rained sometimes

HMP Northward – Uniform Badge

HMP Northward, Grand Cayman

Male Cellblock

Female Cell Block

Vegetable Patch

Chickens Behind Bars

Prison Laundry

Pottery Shop

Selling Prison Products at the Market

CRAFT SALE

Inmates' skill was on display

Story and photos by Carol Winker

Shell earrings, thatch purses and fans, ceramic lotion bottles and drinking mugs, waste baskets and book covers were among the handy and decorative items offered for sale on Friday by Northward Prison staff.

The craft, plus some eggs and ground provisions, were all produced by prison inmates. Money from sales is used to purchase more raw materials for the prison work programme, Principal Officer Tadd Welcome said.

Approximately 50 prisoners take part in various craft groups, with the women concentrating on sewing and weaving. Men do ceramics and wood work. They are paid a wage, as are inmates who work in other areas of the prison.

At least three items on display were not for sale: they were models of a picnic table, swing and bench which the woodshop produces on order under the guidance of Mr. Winston Williamson.

He was on hand to answer questions from potential customers, along with Ms. Annie Morris, who teaches sewing; Ms. Edna Anderson, who handled sales; Principal Officer Gordon Culpin and Mr. Welcome.

Rain on Friday morning slowed sales, but the officers said they intended to apply for permission to have another sale outside the Court House again soon.

Article from the Cayman Compass

Prison Rules

Christmas 1999

🔗 Taken Hostage 🔗

On the 29th of April 1999, at about 09:30hrs, Frank and I were taken hostage with Frank by five Jamaican inmates. It all happened so quickly. I had just returned to my office when an inmate came in and said, "Mr. Marshall wants to see you in his office". Not thinking that this was a unusual request, I went in to find five inmates surrounding me with knives in their hands. They demanded that I sat down behind the desk with Frank. Realising the danger of the situation, I complied with their instructions. At this stage they attempted to put handcuffs on me but could not find the keys. So, I ended up in a chair beside Frank with the desk trapping us against the wall. Apart from going to the toilet, this is where I stayed for the next 28 hours.

For the first few hours it was very confusing, and it was clear the hostage takers had not planned for there to be two of us. When it was 5 to 1 the odds were on their side but with 5 to 2 it was not so good. The two inmates taking the lead were mature criminals, doing nine years, the other three appeared to be going along for the ride. One of three was an inmate who I had developed a good relationship with up to now. This was someone to work on. Frank and I just kept quiet to start with, letting them rant and rave and doing anything they asked. Using the phone in my office the leader spoke to the local priest and asked him to be their spokesman. Their demand appeared to be that all Jamaican prisoners should have equal rights and sentencing procedures to Caymanian prisoners. The priest asked to speak to me and explained he would contact the prison authorities and put their case forward and act as the intermediary. The Director could not have known what was going on as, unknown to me, he was away, and the Deputy Director was acting as head of the prison.

After a few hours little appeared to be happening other than a few phone calls backwards and forwards. The inmate leader kept shouting and making his demands on the phone to someone who appeared to be from the prison service. On one such call I was asked to speak to the caller and make them understand the prisoners' demands. The caller was a prison manager, who wanted to know which room we were being held in, as they were getting ready to break in with guns firing. I explained to the caller that we were in no danger at present and the inmates were showing us respect. Without letting the inmates know what questions I was replying to, I tried to explain that we did not want them to come storming in at this point. I made very clear on the phone, "we do we do not want any tea!", meaning, "No do not come in!" It was clear to me they knew nothing about hostage negotiation and wanted to do it the 'Jamaican way', all guns blazing. At about 10pm, the inmates appeared to be getting nowhere and they started to make threats as to what they would do to us if their demands were not met. Cutting fingers off was mentioned.

It was time to plan my escape. We could not do much while we were wedged behind the desk and in any case, there were always two or more inmates guarding us. We needed to find another opportunity and I realized that when I asked to go to the toilet, I was allowed into the passageway between the two offices to do my business in a bucket. The only guard was one inmate guarding the exit door. Knowing there was a cheap lock on the door, I felt that, if I bent down and rammed the inmates into the door, it would give way and I would fall out into the yard. My only concern was what would they do to Frank if I escaped? A chance I may have to take.

Around this time the inmates had contacted Cell Block Two and were encouraging them to make trouble if their demands were not met. It was clear that the hostage takers had no idea what they were doing and had no clear plan. Time to get to work on them and exploit this lack of preparation. The youngest one always looked frightened when he was on guard duty, so I tried calming him down and asking questions about his family. Was he married? Did he have children? I told him about my family and that I had joined the army when I was 15 years old and trained to kill! One of the other inmates joined in the discussion and before long we were joking about our past experiences.

Nowadays, people ask me if I was frightened, and the answers had got to be, YES. My biggest concern was whether

Wendy knew what was going on. Unknown to me, my photo was on TV and published in the island newspaper, with a story of what was going on. It appeared she knew more than I did. The Police Commissioner's wife, a friend of Wendy's, had come round to the house to give her and Frank's wife support. Nothing appeared to happen for hours at a time. At some point before midnight there had been a large disturbance coming from cell block two, but it had now calm down. After midnight, tea and sandwiches were delivered for us.

Until the early hours it had been difficult for me to communicate with Frank but as the inmates got tired, they were losing concentration on what they were doing, sometimes leaving only one guarding the doorway. This enabled us to talk quietly and plan a way out. While there was only one guarding the doorway, I suggested to Frank that, as I was nearest the door, I could jump up and shut the door. This would leave Frank to drag the table across the room to the door and jamming it, giving us time to smash the window out and escape. Would it work? Well, as it turned out, I will never know. By early morning the inmates appeared to be getting somewhere with the negotiations. They were realising that a peaceful outcome was the sensible solution; not a good time to upset this and try to escape. I thought this was a good time to tell the inmates that we would give them our support to achieve this outcome. To prove our point, I handed over my penknife and Frank's handcuffed keys which has been in our possession all along, as they had never searched us. I told them that we could have got away at any time but had stayed to protect them. They fell for it and, at 2pm, we were released.

After we left the container, we were met by the Police Commissioner and escorted to the gate. On passing the cell blocks we had a lot of banter shouted at us, "It's about time you came out and did some work", all very friendly. The rest of the prison population were also glad it was over as they had been locked up for best part of 20 hours. At the gate we were met by our wives and, after giving Wendy the biggest hug of her life, we had a short de-brief with the Director and government officials as well as some photos for the local paper. Wendy then took me home to a great reunion with her and her parents.

The Director gave us two days off to recover but, the next day, on the way for a meal at our favourite restaurant, I could not resist calling in to the prison to see if there had been any resentment built up against me. I need not have worried because the inmates and staff showed real concern and hoped I would be backed on duty soon. On returning to duty, I found that our office had been moved to a passageway above the gate lodge, well out of harm's way. After a few days the local press printed their version of events. From this I learnt a lot about what had been going on to get our release and the agreements the government had made with the inmates to meet their demands. Copies of these agreements were also published in the paper. One of the things that came out of this was that the inmates involved would only receive the statutory punishments the prison could give, and no further court proceedings would be implemented. This meant that no criminal charges could be brought against the hostage takers. They would not have got away so lightly in the UK, or in most countries, where this serious incident would have been dealt with in the criminal court. Even more frustratingly, they had agreed the punishment without talking to the hostages and understanding what they went through! The outcome was that they all received a further six months added to their existing sentences.

After about two weeks Frank and I received an invitation for us and our wives to have a long weekend break in Jamaica courtesy of the Jamaican community on the island. The hostage takers had been Jamaican nationals and they wanted to show us that not all Jamaicans behaved as these inmates did. We were very grateful and had a wonderful time. Sometime in June, a request was made by the government office for Frank and I and our wives to go to Fort Lauderdale near Miami for psychiatric assessments following the hostage taking. I did not understand what this procedure was, but it was a few days off the island, so we went ahead with it. It required us to attend the university and be interviewed over a two-day period. I was totally confused with what was going on, but the interviewee said they had got some useful information from the interviews and would be able to use it if future events occurred. Later I had the opportunity of reading the report, but thought it was best left unread.

Work was now back to normal, with me getting involved in all aspects of prison life again. One of my duties, only a short time later, was to adjudicate on one of the inmates that had taken me hostage. I suggested that this was not a good idea, but the Director insisted. Since the incident, the five inmates involved had been on maximum security. Fortunately, the adjudication went smoothly. Also in June, the island held a parade for the Queen's birthday, which the Prison service were required to take part in. I volunteered to take part, but my offer was declined, possibly because I would have been the only white man. However, I did take the prison officer contingent on refresher drill training.

In all the time I had been on the island the Director had shown little interest in the prison's development. I suggested that, because there had been no increase in staff for years and the inmate population had almost doubled, it would be a good time to train up some new staff. I had experience of training so they could make good use of my skills. He agreed and asked if I could complete it in two weeks, as funds were very low. My reply was that in the UK all new recruits received nine weeks basic training, but I was willing to compress the training into four weeks. He reluctantly agreed and I proceeded to plan the necessary programme, while he selected up to 20 recruits. Frank had a little training experience, and I would use him to support me.

Fortunately, I had brought my old training manuals with me, so was able to develop a four-week course. It was important that I did not make it too complicated, sticking to the basic skills that a new officer would need. It turned out that the Director could only find ten new recruits. I would use the first week to establish their basic skills levels and establish the way they needed to communicate. It is important that a prison officer can communicate and be understood by inmates. At first, they found it very hard to understand the need for these skills but, with a lot of role playing, they began to understand its importance. Also during the first week, they were measured up for their uniforms.

The second week I concentrated on the other skills a prison officer would need. This included control of inmates' security at all levels, the searching of cells, prison grounds and rub down and strip searching of inmates. When it came to the strip searching, they found it difficult and embarrassing, so to start off I put myself up as an inmate. They soon found it was crucial to stick to the laid down procedures. To make it more realistic I concealed some drugs and a razor blade amongst my clothing. They did not find either and realized how important it was to search thoroughly.

During the third and fourth weeks I continued to repeat the previous training and added report writing, prison rules and regulations, and party control (maintaining security while ensuring the work was done). To help with this I arranged for them to have sessions in the prison shadowing a prison officer at work. During their training I took them on the drill square to smarten them up and teach them to work as a team, warning them that there would be a final passing out parade. Overall, most of the recruits settled down and were keen to take it all in. Halfway through the last week I set them a written examination, to find out what they had really learnt. Eight out of 10 of the recruits passed the standard I had set. Unfortunately, two did not, mainly because their intelligence level was very poor. I suggested they took some English training and reapply at a later date. On the second to last day, they were issued with their uniforms, and they looked very smart. So, after a final rehearsal, the passing out parade took place the next day. The families and friends of the recruits, along with Frank's wife and Wendy were invited to attend the big day. After marching on the parade square, led by me, they were inspected and given a welcome by the Director followed by a march past off the parade square. After the parade the new prison officers presented plaques to Frank and me in appreciation of our hard work, but not a word was said to us by the Director. It had been a lot of work to only get eight new staff and, to make things worse, the Director posted one to the Works Department and the another to the kitchen, a luxury we could not afford! While the training had been going on a new officer had been seconded from the UK. His job was to take over training. This was strange as he had no UK training experience. However, he had been at Northward in the 1980s and so he knew his way around.

Around this time other government departments were negotiating their annual pay increments and I was asked to represent the prison service. It was known to me that both the fire service and the police were on much higher pay rates than the prison staff. At the meeting I stood up and raised the point that the prison service pay rates were unfair. The fire service spokesman replied that his men did a far more important job than we did. My reply was my staff worked from the time they come on duty until the time they go off. "How many fires had been attended to during the last six months", I asked? I also brought up points about the rank structure and was told it would be reviewed. Later in that month, to my surprise, the prison staff had a pay rise, and the rank structure was brought into line with the police. This gave the Director a pay rise of over $6000 a year rise. No complaints from him!

It was now August 1999. In the last month a prisoner, in for murder, had escaped and was on the run. Being only a small island, there was nowhere for him to go, but it still took over 4 weeks to find him. It became apparent to me there was a general unrest in the prison. On making enquiries with inmates, who I had a good relationship with, it was clear overcrowding and the fact that 50 per cent or more were of Jamaican origin were the main causes. Towards the end of September, I was instructed by the Director to adjudicate on a young Caymanian inmate and have him removed to the Behaviour Modification Wing (the old hanging block).

I carried out his instructions but said it may cause a lot of resentment in the prison. The next day, during my evening visit, I was called to the Behaviour Modification Block to find the upstairs section had been barricaded at the top of the stairs. On approaching the top of the stairs, a bowl of water was thrown over me, followed by an apology, they thought I was the Director. I had tried to mediate but they demanded to see the Director, who was sent for. On returning to the lower section, I found the cells damaged and the number of inmates asking to be relocated. As a short-term solution, I located them in the education centre. The Director arrived and spent some time talking to these inmates and, in the early hours of the morning, it all went quiet. I was sent home and returning later, found the incident appeared to be over. I do not know what the Director agreed to, but the wing had been cleaned up, and few of the inmates had been relocated, and all was quiet. I asked for a debrief on the incident to see if there was anything we could learn but was told it was not necessary.

I later found out that a few inmates had been going out the wing in the evening and returning in the early hours of the morning via a roof vent. I was later told that some of the staff knew about it. The roof had been reinforced to stop this and this was said to be the cause of the unrest. Why I had not been informed remains a mystery to this day, like lots of goings on. During this time, and for the rest of that week, Frank was off the island on holiday. Given what was about to happen, this was lucky for him!

New Recruits on Parade

Ready for service... The new recruits pose for a commemorative shot with prison director Eric Smith (front, centre right), who is flanked by training officers Gordon Culpin (right) and Frank Marshall (left). *Photos: GIS*

Report in the local newspaper

⛓ Riot ⛓

On the 30th of September 1999 the prison went into total meltdown, meaning a riot. It was about 9.00am, I was working in my office, when I heard a lot of shouting and the smell of burning. Looking out the passage window I could see a lot of inmates running about the grounds and in and out of the buildings. They were dressed, for want of a word, like pirates, with head bands and homemade spears. My first thoughts were that I did not want to be part of this, and my nerves started to get the better of me. For a short while all I wanted to do was get away. However, when another manager came to me for help, because he could not find the directors, I forgot my fears and started organising the staff. All the staff had left the inside of the prison and were hanging about the gate area awaiting instructions. My first thoughts were to contain the situation, so I sent some staff to man the perimeter fence and report any attempts to escape. Next, I reported the situation to the police and asked for their assistance. By this time many of the wooden buildings, including the education, stores, canteen and laundry, were engulfed in flames. Inmates who did not want to be involved came to the gate asking to be let out. At about midday, most of the inmates were hiding behind the buildings, so

Riot

I decided to go in with 10 officers and find out what their problems were.

I stood in the main square under the flagpole flying the Cayman Island Flag and called for a leader to come out. I was quickly confronted by about 50 shouting inmates. I asked one of the inmates who I knew very well what was this all about. He said it was very confusing and that there were several small groups fighting each other with no one objective. He advised me to return to the gate for my own safety. On looking around me, I realized that the other officers had already retreated to the gate. I was standing there all on my own! So, I took his advice and retreated. As there was no sign of any of the Directors, I took it upon myself to organize the staff. All available staff were called in and I set up security posts around the outside of the fence. By this time all the staff had been accounted for and I knew they were safe. I observed from an upstairs window that a lot of the inmates involved in the disturbance were going into the stores dressed like rioters and coming out dressed in new uniforms; asking to be let out as if they were not part of the riot.

The police arrived in force around midday, mostly armed with guns. I spoke to the Deputy Police Commissioner and told him what had happened and what we had done so far. The Fire Service had also arrived and were trying to put building fires out by spraying water over from outside the fence. We agreed that we needed to relocate some of the prisoners to a safer location. Up to now, the female section had not been involved in the disturbances, but information was coming to me that some of the inmates were trying to get into the female compound. The police arranged for a hole to be cut in the fence at the rear and all 29 females were taken out and relocated at a civic hall in Bodden Town, a few miles away. To reduce the male population, about 50 low category inmates were taken to the East End Village Hall.

All this movement depleted my staff availability, so we were given support by the police; on overtime pay no doubt! By this time the remaining prisoners had quietened down and were mostly hiding away, so the police decided to go into the main compound with their guns. After one shot was fired, they quickly withdrew. The police had fired over the heads of the inmates because they thought they had seen someone with a gun. Up to now the prison staff had overseen the situation, but it was clear to me that we did not have the resources to cope. The Directors were nowhere to be seen and in fact I never saw them again. It was agreed with the police that they would take over control of the prison, and the prison staff would assist wherever they could. I formed up all the staff up in the gate lodge and praised them for what they had done so far and ask them to give the police as much support as possible.

For the next few hours, it was a very confusing time, both inside and out. Families of the inmates had got to hear of the situation and were crowding outside seeking information on their loved ones. During a quiet period, the police went inside and arrested the ringleaders, one of whom turned out to be one of the five inmates who took me hostage, along with the main ringleader who was serving life for murder of a prison officer. They were relocated in George Town police station cells, awaiting transfer to a UK prison. It was clear from what the inmates were saying that most of the accommodation was badly damaged. The main kitchen and food store had been ransacked and all the appliances put out of action. There were around 200 inmates left in the prison and, by early evening, the fires were mainly out, and the situation was calming down. Inmates were looking for food and somewhere to sleep. They were told they would have to make do with what they could find until the next day.

A meeting was held by the police, which I attended, to discuss the way forward. I was instructed to maintain a staff shift pattern of 12 hours on and 12 hours off. A local restaurant was contracted to provide three meals a day delivered to the gate for all inmates. A hatch was made in the inner gate to pass the food to inmates during mealtimes. A temporary medical centre was set up inside the gate lodge area to deal with injury and sickness. The outer fence guard was doubled up with the help of armed police. Inmates were informed that, if they tried to escape, they would be shot.

In the early hours of the morning, I went home for a well-earned rest, returning at first light to find that the prison looked like a bomb site. The prison appeared to have remained quiet and most of the prisoners had found

Riot

somewhere to sleep. Now that most of the agitators had been removed, there was a need to restore some sort of order. A role check was important, as it was possible that some may have been killed. A partial check was made when inmates collected their meals from the gate, but when there was food not all came. So, with the permission of the police, I went in with another officer, aided by an inmate, to do a role check. It took nearly 2 hours, but I was able to account for everyone. It was clear the inmates were sleeping all over the place, some 50 in the church, 30 in the hospital and a lot more in makeshift shelters. A few gangs had been set up, mainly to protect themselves. Overall, most inmates knew they were going to have to return to the old rules and appeared keen to help rebuild the prison.

Frank had just got back from his stay off the island and could not believe what he saw. For the next week or so a daily routine was set up, three meals a day, daily medical checks and I continued to go in to do a daily roll check and spend more and more time inside the prison, reassuring the inmates and letting them know what was going to happen next. Most of the inmates were happy to talk to me, but when the local staff went in, they were not very co-operative. The government had allocated two million dollars for a rebuild. As this would only cover the materials inmates would be required to do the work. After seeing them build a church, which they had done a year or so before with the aid of a local builder, I knew they were capable. We were turning back to a real prison again.

Riot

In late October, Sir Stephen Tumin was nominated to carry out a full report on the disturbances and riots over the last six months. I knew of him as he had been the Chief Inspector of prisons in the 1970s and 1980s, and I had met him when he did an inspection of Dover Borstal. On his first day on the island, he requested an interview with me and asked me to put in my own words what had happened and the probable reasons. I had an interesting 3-hour discussion where I pulled no punches. The whole prison was unfit for purpose. The Directors had not got the experience to run a prison of this size and complexity. They just played lip service to the government and hoped they would get away with it. A complete overhaul was needed, to include the prison buildings, separation of the different categories of prisoners, and total re-training of staff. To achieve this, I suggested an experienced UK prison governor be seconded, along with around 20 prison officers to support and train the local staff. For example, up to now security had been a bit of a joke. Security keys were handed round like locker keys with no one being responsible. HMP Northward needed to be brought into the 21st century. I have since read the full report and and was pleased to see that many of my suggestions were included as recommendations. Although I agreed with a lot of what was said in the report, I still felt that it lacked some credibility as to the real facts.

It was about this time that a Caymanian Principal Officer, Mrs. Range, was put in charge of the prison staff. What she

Riot

did is a mystery to me as I seldom saw her in the prison as her office was outside the fence. On several occasions I had tried contacting her to offer her my full support but got nowhere. I felt she resented me being at the prison, probably because I was not from the island and was a man. She had no experience of running a prison, having only been in the service a few years. As a rule, most government departments were run by islanders irrespective of their ability to do the job. On several occasions when I was doing weekend duties, I found an extra member of staff on duty. When I asked what he was doing his reply was always, "work for Mrs. Range". I later found out that he was monitoring me and reporting back to Mrs. Range. When I queried his presence Mrs Range confirmed, "he's doing extra work for me".

A government minister was put in charge of the rebuild and allocating funds for the refurbishment. This started with the accommodation and kitchen as a high priority, and the inmates played a big part in the rebuild. As I had found before, there was a lot of skill waiting to be put to good use. For some time now I had suspected that the dealings between the prison management and government were not all above board, but up to now could not prove it. When the new UK governor came out, I warned him about my suspicions and continued to pass on any information that I received from the inmates. I also suggested he read all documents carefully before signing them. As an example, new washing machines were ordered to be placed outside the accommodation blocks until a new laundry could be built. Twenty were ordered but only three arrived at the prison. Information received from a reliable inmate indicated that the others had been delivered to the family and friends of government ministers. I felt I would have to start watching my back, as I got the feeling that those in power could be out to get me if I did not go with the flow. I judged that it was a case of either turning a blind eye to corruption or get out. They did not understand that being open and honest was the way I work, both with staff and prisoners alike.

It was time to take a break, so Wendy and I went to Cuba for a few days and had a great time. On return and before Christmas 1999 the UK seconded officers started to arrive, a few at a time. After some induction training, I spread them about the accommodation blocks with clear instructions to work with and not take over from local staff. They soon settled down and their experience was appreciated by the local staff. Over the next few months big improvements were carried out at the prison. A new security fence was put up and the old female wing was converted to be used by privilege status male inmates. The old Behaviour Modification Block, or D wing as it was now called, was converted into a maximum-security wing with a large two storey extension. The works and stores department were relocated to an area in the outside car park.

Frank and I now occupied the old Deputy Director's office. Our roles had now been reversed and I now became responsible for security; a role I felt should have done from the very beginning. There were lots to do, and I could not wait to get started. With my security background I was able to prioritise the work. All security locks were replaced with new Chubb locks and for the first-time staff would be accountable for their own keys. A safe was fitted in the inner lodge gate and keys were issued in exchange for a numbered tally which corresponded to an individual member of staff. Just like a real prison. With the two staff I was allocated, a new security programme was introduced which included daily outer and inner fence checks, checks of locks, bolts and bars on all accommodation wings with a full record kept and random drug tests were also increased. I introduced updated training sessions with a few staff at a time and told them security was the most important part of their work and, if done correctly, could protect them and their fellow colleagues. As there were now three other locations around the Island where prisoners were held, I had to make regular visits to them all to ensure a high standard of security was being kept. I developed a good relationship with the new Director and he often called me up to ask my advice.

It was now coming up for my second Christmas on the island our son came out during his holidays from university, so I was able to spend some time diving with him in blue Caribbean seas. We booked a Christmas lunch at a beach hotel and had a wonderful time. The millennium New Year was now upon us, and we were invited to the home of a friend of Wendy's for the celebration. They had a mansion on the beach, very posh! They even employed a chef to come over from France to prepare a banquet. We had a great time which went on into the early hours of the morning.

Back at work the prison was slowly recovering and the rebuild neared completion. The female inmates were still located in the village hall at East End of the Island. With the role down to twenty-five, it was not ideal, but would have to do in the short term. The low category male inmates had for some time been located in what they called Tent City. This had been a part-built hospital on the edge of George Town, which had been used previously as a refugee camp for Cubans. It had a large fence surrounding it which it made an ideal location. The long-term plans were to convert this camp into a female prison.

During January the government set up several planning groups called Vision 2008. Their aim was to plan and agree the way forward to where they would like to be in 2008. As they could not find anyone to represent the Prison Service, I agreed to attend the Zero Tolerance for Crime and Drugs Group. The group was made up mainly of islanders with me, the police Commissioner and a probation officer. We met once a week for three months and had some lively discussions. The locals on the group wanted no crime on the island but could not understand that to achieve this they would have to play their part. For example, by reporting misdemeanours by their family and friends to the police. They expected the police to deal with all the problems and it took some time to convince them that everyone had to be involved. At the end of three months, a strategic plan was drawn up and submitted to the government ministers. What came out of it I never found out as I had left the island before the final decision was made.

A new Governor from the UK was appointed for a two-year period to start in May 2000. D block was nearing completion and as security manager I was asked to inspect the building. There were a lot of small security hazards, such as cell doors and gates opening outwards and could be used to block the passageways. The cell window bars were very weak and needed strengthening. The walls in the exercise yard had square corners and with some effort an inmate could wedge himself against the sides and work himself to the top. However, it was a great improvement on the old buildings.

During February 2000 I had to make up my mind whether I was going to sign on for another two years. The Director wanted me to stay and, as I was now an Assistant Director, he felt I could play an important role in the continuing improvements of the prison. After long discussions with Wendy, being aware that this was her life as well and she enjoyed the island life, we agreed to stay, on the condition we move to a luxury apartment close to the beach. Much of my work now kept me office bound, planning new security systems, staff shift patterns and arranging the necessary staff training. Meanwhile, Mrs. Range had been appointed Deputy Director, not bad with only six years prison experience! I found it hard to work with her and often disagreed with her plans but, as she would be the Director in a few years, I had to go along with her.

We found a brand-new apartment close to the beach within our price range and could take it over in May. As I was overdue my annual leave, we arranged a flight back to the UK for a few weeks in April. It was about then, that I began finding out about more and more irregularities going on with the prison rules being bent to suit the island staff. I asked myself, do I want two more years of this? I was losing my courage, probably due to the hostage and riot situations. As I was not the type who could just sit back and let the world go by, I felt it was likely I would make myself ill or I would be fitted up with some false charges and end up in prison myself. So, when the time came that I had to sign over the new apartment, I more or less broke down told Wendy that I was sorry, but I could not work anymore in this environment. We agreed we would have to leave the island.

I informed the Director and Minister of Prisons of my intentions and asked for the necessary arrangements to be made. Once the decision was made it was like a weight off my shoulders. I continued to work my last two months out, where possible, completing any project I had been involved in. My replacement arrived about three weeks before I was due to leave. A strange choice! He had been to the island the year before to run a control and restraint course for staff at this prison and from other British West Indian prisons. As far as I was aware he had little prison management experience. But this was not my problem anymore.

In the last week Wendy, I moved out of our apartment and into a hotel. We hired a car for a few days, as we had sold our two cars, and packed any property we were sending back to the UK. During our stay on the island Wendy had made a lot of good friends, several of whom we are still in contact with, and we invited them all to a farewell party at a friend's house. At the beginning of May 2000, we said goodbye to the island, and with some regrets flew home.

Some years later we met up with Frank, who had stayed for a further four years. It was apparent that little had changed HMP Northward. It was just muddling through from year to year.

Farewell to Cayman

🔗 Back Home 🔗

I was back in Folkestone where I had started my working life and now nearly 60-year-old. What was I going to do with myself? I was too young to give up work completely and still had an inkling to work in a private sector prison. These were prisons built and run by private companies. Was I totally mad after what I had been through or did I have a few more years left in me? Well, I gave it ago. In January 2001 I joined Premier Prisons at a new prison nearing completion in Staffordshire, called HMP Dovegate. My role was to be the Security Manager.

When I started only a few managers had been employed. The Governor was from the public sector prison service and had left under a cloud. The two deputy governors had never worked in the prison sector before. There were also two other managers who had, like me, retired from the public sector. Quite a mixed bag. The Governor's expectations were very high, and he just piled on the work, day after day. When I asked for staff to assist me, I was told just get on with. A new training officer joined the team with instructions to train all the new staff as they arrived. This was going to be quite difficult as he had just retired from the RAF and had no knowledge of prison service training. I offered him some of my experience but was told it was nothing to do with me. After three months it was clear that I was totally mad to consider this job. I spoke to the Governor with my concerns, and he replied, "we only employed you for your experience, it's this or nothing". So, I handed in my resignation and left. They just want to get the job done on the cheap.

This really was the end of my life behind bars. I did not need this type of pressure at my time in life. Still eager to work I got the job as a part time school caretaker. As it happened this school was a descendant of the school, I had attended in the 1950s. It had just changed its name and location several times. It suited me well, no management pressure and a chance to use my practical skills again and have a laugh and joke with the pupils along the way. Working only 30 hours a week gave me plenty of time for my other interests. At times I was asked to look after unruly pupils who could not be sent home due to not being able to contact their parents. Was this a touch of a borstal officer? I would tell the pupils, "if you're with me you must work". In fact, sometimes pupils would ask to work with me rather than attend their classes. The head teacher was happy to let me use my DIY skills; painting and decorating, repairing locks and toilets and general maintenance. The fire alarms were something I was responsible for. When they went off the school had to be cleared and I had to check all areas. This could be a regular task as the alarms were often set off by pupils.

Back Home

I remember once walking past a classroom and seeing hot tar dripping from the ceiling, the teacher was just carrying on. When I ask why she had not evacuated the class she said, "I have not been told too". As there was hot tar dripping on some of the desks, I gave her the instruction. Later in the day a fire started on the roof, the school was evacuated, and I locked all the external doors to stop anyone returning. When the Fire service came, they were about to smash all the doors down. I produced the keys stopping them doing a job they love. When they were running out the hoses, I offered to help. The fire officer could not keep up with me and explained that he was 59 years old. I was 63 at the time. Another time a small fire started in the science room which I put out with an extinguisher. When the firemen arrived, they told me it was their job to put out fires!

After about 18 months Wendy and I decided to move away from Kent and, after a lot of searching, found a beautiful bungalow in a small village in Lincolnshire. It had 1/4 acre of garden so no need to go out to work, or so I thought. Soon after we moved Wendy got a new job as a Registrar for births and deaths and marriages. A job she wished she had done all her working life. Maybe I would get a part time job? On looking through the local paper I saw an advertisement for a gardener handyman in a village nearby. On attending an interview, I found the garden was a 40-acre farm with a huge farmhouse, lots of outbuildings, a large duck pond and a walled garden. The owner let out most of the farm for grazing horses. He ran an overseas company teaching mine clearance and dealing with hostage situations on aircraft. He offered me the job two days a week for £7 per hour. As the minimum wage at the time was £5 per hour, I was questioning why would he pay more? I told him I would let him know later. After thinking it over I phoned him and explain my concerns. His reply was that he had interviewed several people for this post, but I was the one he wanted. He went on to explain that the farm and buildings were used for SAS training and my security experience would be ideal. I worked for him for over a year. Then he sold his training company and did not need my services anymore.

My next and last paid job was with a care home just 400 yards over a field from my home, where I was employed as a gardener and handyman. The care home was a falling down old mill house with large gardens and a rare breed birds centre in the grounds. This turned out to be a very interesting job. I was often asked to work with patients suffering from various learning difficulties. They would help me build aviaries for the rare birds and general gardening work. There was also a cage for small monkeys. They bred regularly, so I had to keep extending their living accommodation. What great fun I had with them, going in the cage and letting them run all over me. They loved marshmallows. I was also nominated to be the staff member responsible for health and safety. This required me checking the fire alarm and hot water temperatures every month and making sure the paths, stairs and pathways were safe.

It was now 2006 and I was coming up for 65 years old. Wendy was the Treasurer of the local village hall, and I was Vice-Chairman of the local bowls club. We had really settled down to life in the country. However, Wendy's ageing parents were having more and more health problems, which required us to go backwards and forwards to Kent, a 500-mile round trip. So, with great regret, we sold up and moved back to Folkestone. I had now reached the end of my paid working life. From that day until now I only do voluntary work.

When I look back at my working life, I am very proud of my achievements. I think the time I spent in the prison service was the highlight of my career. Strange as it may seem I enjoyed working with criminals, especially the young offenders to whom I felt I had a lot to offer. A high percentage of prisoners are young and in prison for the first time. I thought they should be given a chance. A lot came from disrupted families or none. Guidance and training are what most of them needing what I call life experience. This is what I endeavoured to pass on all my working life behind bars. Without my other experiences, would I have done as well? No. The army had made a man of me and had given me the confidence to make the best of what was put in front of me, for the whole rest of my working life.

Milton Keynes UK
Ingram Content Group UK Ltd.
UKHW020219310823
427765UK00011B/195